LIFE'S MOST CRITICAL QUESTIONS: GOD'S ANSWERS

DR. BETTYE LUNDQUIST

3 TREES
PUBLISHING

3Trees Publishing

18024 Dedeaux Clan Road

Gulfport, MS 39503

3TreesPublishing@gmail.com

CONTENTS

INTRODUCTION

Only God knows the answers to life's most critical questions. I have searched His Word for answers like a miner digging for gold. I will keep looking because revelations are reserved for those who patiently look and dig deeply.

Now I am hearing the LORD say that some of you would like to join me in deep digs.

Perhaps you can find a multitude of treasures that I have missed. Then you can share your treasures with others. And I can share with you. If you are interested, welcome to the dig! If not, I bless you and the different path He has for you.

Whatever path you follow, please listen just a few more minutes for my advice: **"Do not skip the Words of God quoted, thinking that you already know it all." No! The**

Word is alive. One personal, anointed <u>now-word</u> from God can change your whole life.

God has a supernatural habit of ordering what He calls "Kairos" time so that the nugget of truth and wisdom is mined and put in our hands at exactly the right time. Let me give you some valuable nuggets of revelation for our journey:

- Are you aware that each of us has both a godly and a satanic birth assignment?
- Your life's choices will determine which path you choose.
- Choices also determine who walks with you and whose voice you listen to - God's or Satan's.
- And eternally, your choices determine who wins the prize of your eternal life.

That revelation is critical. So, then you must find the right map. Our treasure map will be the Word of God. We must follow this map carefully, since we know there are two totally opposing spiritually mapped paths we could follow. One path leads to eternal life and one ends in destruction and eternal death. The most harrowing turns on our road to eternity are found in the closest calls with Satan's best laid plans! Consider the cross of Jesus and the resurrection as our perfect example. Satan had a birth assignment planned for Jesus and thought he had won through His death on the cross. But he never saw the supernatural resurrection coming.

God's birth assignments are infinitely supernatural! And Satan's best laid plans always kill, steal and destroy. But Satan totally fails when we bow to God and escape his plan.

Trek with me throughout this book as we look at the continual battle between Satan and God over every life and nation.

Satan has not given up, not by a long shot! But he is the eternal loser! We will be carefully studying what is ahead. Join me as we dig all the way to the last word in the Book of Revelation. Let's journey together. One can put a thousand enemies to flight, but two can put ten thousand!

Let's search for **Life's Most Critical Questions: God's Answers in these chapters:**

Who Is God?
Who Am I?
Why Am I Here?
Who Is My enemy?
What Is His Strategy?
How Can I Win?

Hold on to our LORD! Here we go!

1

WHO IS GOD?

Of the six critical questions I opened with in the Introduction, there could be none more critical than "Who Is God?" and our personal answer will surely have eternal consequences. Come with me on a journey into the supernatural, for we can never find the true God any other way! **Father God, open our spiritual eyes and ears to see and hear truth straight from You.**

There are thousands or maybe millions of answers in the world to this question, and as many supernatural beings who want you and I to believe and worship them as our God. But the eternally critical issue is that only One is actually the true God. All the others are liars who will spend eternity in the Lake of Fire. And so will everyone worldwide who believes and worships a counterfeit.

The Bible Clearly Teaches that There Is Only One God

This is the most important principle of the Bible and the theme is not hard to find. I found 28 different passages that clearly state this as fact. See a few below that represent the whole:

Deuteronomy 4:35, 39-40 NASB

"...the LORD, He is God; there is no other besides Him... Know therefore today, and take it to your heart, that the LORD, He is God in heaven above and on earth below; there is no other, so you shall keep His ... commandments... that it may go well with you and with your children...."

Nehemiah 9:6 NASB

"You alone are the LORD. You have made the heavens. the heaven of heavens with all their host, the earth and all that is on it, the seas and all that is in them. You give life to all of them and the heavenly host bows down before You."

When Jesus was asked to teach the disciples what the most important commandment of all is, He answered,

Mark 12:29 The Message

"... Which is the most important of all the commandments?" Jesus said, "The first in importance is, 'Listen Israel: The Lord your God is one, so love the Lord God with all your passion and prayer and intelligence and energy.' And here is the second:

'Love others as well as you love yourself." There is no other commandment that ranks with these."*

Revelation 4:11 NASB

"Worthy are You, our Lord and our God, to receive glory and honor and power; for You created all things, and because of Your will they existed, and were created." Perfect love eternally exists as Father, Son and Holy Spirit, YHWH Elohim.[1]

So, Who Is this One and Only God?

In my life, one very personal revelation of God, sums up and towers above all the rest as preeminent: **God is love!** Love is not just a concept or feeling for me, but the very personal one and only true God! For as long as I can remember, He has made sure that I know Him as Love.

Of course, I want to know much more about Him, and there is much more to know; but this one overwhelming reality is all I have really needed. In the face of His arch enemy who has tried to make my life hell from conception, He has always won my heart and saved my life, so I learned that *"Love never fails."* Absolutely nothing could ever convince me otherwise. **As I unfold my personal story, you will learn that I have also known Satan very well, even**

---

1.   YHWH Elohim is the Hebrew name of the one true creator God introduced in Genesis and made up of three in one Trinity: God, the Father, God the Son, (Yeshua in Hebrew, whom we have called Jesus) and God the Holy Spirit.

from the womb! Perhaps that is why God's love is so real and indisputable to me.

God's love, "agape" in Hebrew, is uniquely supernatural and absolutely the opposite to what our world very tragically calls love. Agape love is infinitely powerful and He is the one and only source. No other "god" has agape love to give, and no human can express true love to anyone without God's indwelling empowerment of true love within him.

Open your heart and allow God to penetrate you with the greatest gift – His love. The Bible beautifully unfolds the awesome revelation of the one true God, Creator of all, YHWH Elohim. **He exists in three persons: God the Father, God the Son and Bridegroom, and God the Holy Spirit.** Perfect Love is demonstrated completely through all three parts of YHWH.

In the beginning, He created all the heavens and the earth, plants and animals perfectly in harmony with each other, and called it good. Then He climaxed all this beauty and magnificence with the creation of man in His own image and likeness, breathing into him and making him a living, unique being that could relate to Him personally. God called him Adam. He breathed into Adam and made him like no other creature, able to know God intimately, and capable of responding to God's love.

Next, He gave him purpose and placed him on the earth to rule and reign with YHWH Elohim Himself as his God. But for the first time, God was not satisfied with his creation of Adam, saying that this creation was not good alone! So, from Adam's rib, He fashioned Eve, the first woman, created to be one flesh with Adam, ruling and reigning together with him, equally yoked in marriage, ordained by God. They were perfectly suited for one another and lived completely safe, vulnerable, naked and unashamed, ruling over the Earth together under YHWH Elohim's direction. They were in perfect unity with each other and all of creation, as God had planned for eternity.

Before his wife was created, YHWH had given Adam one law to obey in order to live forever with no sin and no death. God's one commandment was to not eat of one specific tree–the tree of the knowledge of good and evil. Adam could eat of every other tree, but that one. God's warning was that if Adam ate of that forbidden tree, he would surely die. The wording of this warning in the original language indicated that it was not just to Adam personally, but to mankind, even though at that time, Adam had no idea there would ever even be another human on earth.

During that time, Adam was also given a huge and awesome responsibility to take dominion over the whole earth under YHWH Elohim's authority as supreme ruler. He had given him the one law; then He gave Adam responsibility. **He was to cultivate and keep the garden. The word "keep" means to be the watchmen, hedge the garden around and not let any any enemy in. He was responsible to keep the garden safe from any intruder or danger. Since he was the only human at the time, Adam was held supremely responsible. However, the word mankind was also used here. This is important, because Eve and all of mankind who have been created since** then, also became responsible to rule and reign over God's enemies on earth, and keep them out of our realms of authority. Many years later, David reinforces this point in a different way:

Psalms 115:16 NASB

"The heavens are the heavens of the LORD, but the earth He has given to the sons of man."

Ponder this biblical reality! Look again at what He is saying. Mankind was created to have dominion over this earth in total obedience to God. This fact means that **man, and not God, is to blame for all the evil tolerated on earth!** I was never taught that in church. Wow! That is the bad news and shifts my whole mindset about my responsibilities, even about the horrible evil happening in our nation today. **Are we expecting God to do what he gave us authority and responsibility to do?**

Can you imagine why Father God wanted us to be His sons and daughters in charge of the whole earth? I honestly can't. Frankly, my finite human mind says that He made a really bad decision when He created us with a free will. But He didn't ask me for my opinion and He obviously doesn't agree! Just for my records, here are my facts that have substantiated my opinion: we betrayed Him horribly when He created us humans to be perfect and live experiencing perfect love forever. We were designed to never know sin or death. That was the plan of our God, who is perfect love. Our environment He created was perfect. Adam and Eve's marriage was perfect, and they had been given the perfect whole earth to rule and reign over forever.

They were instructed to start in the garden of Eden that God Himself had planted for them. Can you imagine that perfect relationship with God, walking and talking with God Himself in the cool of the evening? Can you envision the beauty and the joy in a perfect marriage between two perfect people created just for each other?

Knowing how much fun it is just to go to a zoo and see all the awesome animals, can you imagine the garden characterized with peace, safety, and fun with all kinds of animals who never hurt one another or you, plus the beauty of all the flowers and trees and the delicious food he provided? In case you didn't know, everyone, including the animals, were vegetarian in the beginning.[2]

This atmosphere is an example of God's love He created for mankind. He will again allow us to enjoy this in the end, described in the book of Revelation. The joy of His creation minus death will characterize the new heavens and new earth for all believers in Jesus, the Messiah at the time of the end. More details about that later. **All of creation on earth was in perfect harmony, and at perfect peace with each other, God Himself and all of creation.**

As I said Adam was instructed to be the watchman who kept the enemy out of the garden, even before Eve was created. He was told to take dominion, ruling and reigning over the whole earth in perfect, eternal peace.

---

2. Genesis 1:30

Since these promises and commands were given to mankind, and not just to Adam, we assume he told Eve. Ultimately, they were to be fruitful and multiply so their family could inhabit and rule the whole earth. Their God-given destiny was perfect, as only our God could have planned it. But free will! This free will thing seems to be the problem!

They only had one law to obey, one tree not to eat of. But they both blew it all for all of us! If Adam had been the watchman he was destined to be and kept the serpent out of the garden; and if they had not sinned by eating of the forbidden tree, all of this would have lasted for eternity and death would've never touched anyone in God's perfect creation.[3]

Our God knew everything mankind would do from the beginning! Nothing surprises Him! He is omniscient, all knowing! He knew that if He gave us free will, we, just like Adam Eve, would sin and fall and defile His whole creation. One thing is for sure: He did not create us to go to hell with the serpent Satan who led Adam and Eve astray.

Why would He risk all this loss to give us free will? Why? Ok! Now I see! Why haven't I seen this before? He didn't want robots for His sons and daughters or for His Son's bride because robots can't love!

He would have had to create us as programmed robots to prevent our ability to sin! Wow! I'm sorry I sinned and

---

3. Genesis 1-2

caused Jesus to have to die for me on the cross, but I surely am glad I'm not a robot with no free will. Wouldn't it be horrible not to be able to love?

He created us in His image and likeness to be able to love Him like He loves us, and Jesus proved His love and saved our eternal lives on the cross. Our Creator is certainly nothing like a robot.

He is the Perfect Father, the full manifestation of Perfect Love, who desires His children to grow up to be the Beloved Bride for His Son. He wants His family to be filled with Holy Spirit gifts and power.

Empowered by Jesus and Holy Spirit, living in us and working through us, we will be able to supernaturally build His kingdom. We can offer our children eternal life with the only true God.

Our God genuinely wants His family created in His supernatural image. To guarantee this true love relationship, He had to give us a choice. Every man and woman must choose either harlotry with His arch enemies or a true love relationship with Him. You can't have both. To choose any other god will result in your spending eternity in hell with that god, who is actually a fallen angel or demon!

It is at this point in our reasoning that we come to the shocking realization of what God's love truly is and how dramatically different it is from our twisted mindsets about love. **The world's mindset about "love" is harlotry, motivated by what you can get from the other person. Yet biblical God-centered love is all about giving to the**

other person what he or she needs! Boy, does man need God and people who are empowered by His love. Without Him, we would all be bound for hell.

God created man with full knowledge that tragedy was coming because of free will. He knew that man would betray Him and fall into the hands of Satan. He also knew that nobody could save mankind, but Jesus. Jesus would have to humble Himself and become a man, live a perfect life on earth and shed His perfect blood as a sacrifice by dying on a cruel cross. Only He could resurrect from the grave to pay the price for man's salvation. Then and only then could He save mankind from eternal hell. Nobody but Jesus could be that totally pure blood sacrifice necessary to pay in full for our sin.

If God wanted love relationships with mankind as Father's sons and daughters, a bride, for Jesus and Spirit filled new creations to work with Holy Spirit, this was the only possible path. Fully understanding all of that, and the cost to Him, He still created man!

That decision cost Jesus the unfathomable price of the cross. The price for us was paid in full by the sinless blood of Jesus! After the resurrection, **Jesus spent 40 days with His followers, demonstrating to them that the resurrection was real, opening their understanding and preparing them for a whole new era. He had told them that He must leave so Holy Spirit power could come.**

They did not yet know that this encounter with Holy Spirit, called the baptism in the Holy Spirit, would transform them into new creations, never seen before. He was

calling them to their new assignment to go to the whole world and make disciples, so they were going to need new supernatural power and gifting.[4]

Then it was time for the resurrected Jesus to go to the right hand of the Father[5] to prepare for the incredible shift ahead. He was preparing to rule and reign as the Head of the Church which was about to be born through their baptism in the Holy Spirit. Jesus said that He must go, so Holy Spirit could come[6] and empower them.

The Kingdom of God must operate with the most awesome supernatural power ever known to mankind. This shift was absolutely necessary to transform and empower His disciples by God, the Holy Spirit to take the world back from the evil one. Has the church of today understood our assignment and power to accomplish our destiny? I don't think so!

Religion is one of the chief enemies of God because it is the deceptive counterfeit of God's Kingdom. After the

---

4. As I am making the statement, I wonder if that is not the main issue in our world today? How many Christians truly understand that it is our lack of manifesting the power of Holy Spirit against the supernatural wickedness manifesting all around us that is our primary problem in the church and around the world today? And innumerable numbers of angel armies are at our disposal to defeat and remove wicked spirits in high places. Just like Satan was in the garden evil spirits attack our "gardens." But who truly believes that and is calling on angelic help? How about you and me? We are totally responsible to find out why we are here for such a time is this, just as responsible as Adam was in the garden! He was responsible in the beginning, but we are just as responsible as we move closer to the end!

5. Ephesians 1:9 – 2:6

6. John 16:7

resurrection of Jesus and the baptism of His believers in the Holy Spirit, as new creations, they ruled and reigned both in Him as His body and with Him in the third heaven at the right hand of Father God. They also manifested His kingdom on earth with power and great glory. Everything changed, and the Kingdom of God was now operating in fullness with Jesus as the Head and believers as His body. Over the years, much has been stolen and counterfeited in the church world-wide.

Yet the entire Trinity is still summing everything up in Christ Jesus. They are preparing for the New Jerusalem to come down and function as the New Heaven and the New Earth together in the end times. Those days are probably closer than we think. But how many will believe and be saved and how many will be deceived and eternally lost?

Our three in one God: Father, Son and Holy Spirit, knew all along that we would cost Him the supreme price of being ripped apart to save and deliver us from our foolish and sinful choices. Only then could we be redeemed into His family. What a price YWHW Elohim, the one and only true God, paid for us! I told you that God is Agape Love.

Agape Love Does Not Exist Apart From God
1 John 4:7-11 NASB

"Beloved, let us love one another, for love is from God; and everyone who loves is born of God and knows God. The one who does not love, does not know God, for God is love. By this, the love of God was manifested in us, that God has sent His only

begotten son into the world so that we might live through Him. And this is Love, not that we loved God, but that He loved us and sent His son to be the propitiation for our sins. Beloved, if God so loved us, we ought also love one another."

God's love is unconditional and eternal for all of His creation! He is not like us. He loves us so much. He gives us what we truly need and not what we foolishly or even demonically desire, no matter the cost to Him. Agape love is a supernatural God thing! You will never find agape love anywhere else. As we have just seen, the greatest example in all of human history is the cross of Jesus Christ, where Perfect Love died to pay in full for all our sins so we would not spend eternity in hell with Satan and all the fallen angels, but with Him in a perfect love relationship forever.

All Through the Bible
God Revealed Himself to Man
Through His Names
Manifested Through
Supernatural Encounters

Each of the biblical stories, revealing His names is worthy of a chapter, but I will just share an abbreviated list of His names, hoping you will search the word for the whole story. He often starts His name with **YHWH. In Hebrew, that name means "I Am." He is saying "I Am whoever you need Me to be!" Example: "You need healing? I Am YHWH Rapha, God, your Healer."** I pray that just reading this partial list will encourage and bless you.

Know Him by His Names

Our God is YHWH Elohim, Father, Son, Holy Spirit, The Alpha and the Omega, the Beginning and the End, Messiah, Deliverer, Immanuel, God With Us, Abba Father, Comforter, Friend, The Good Shepherd, The Way, The Truth, The Life, The Light of the World, YHWH Rapha, God My Healer, King of Kings, LORD of Lords, My Beloved, Ishi, My Husband, Balm of Gilead, Prince of Peace, Mighty God, Wonderful Counselor, Jehovah Jireh, My Provider, The Bridegroom, Everlasting Father, The Resurrection and the Life, The Lamb of God, Son of David, Son of Abraham, Son of God, The Almighty, Son of Man, El Roi, The God Who Sees, The Gift, Christ the Lord and at least hundreds more. Each Name has a great meaning in the Bible as He revealed it personally and intimately. Perhaps He has introduced Himself to you personally, too. When He does, you never forget it because God encounters are intimate and life changing.

I hope you understand by now that the one and only God did not create you to miss the most important eternal relationship in your life. If you cultivate that relationship no matter how horrible human relationships are, and how badly you are treated, you will always experience perfect love that lasts forever and deepens constantly. I bless you with this most precious love that exists.

I want to climax the short revelation of our God, who is Perfect Love with two totally supernatural true stories - one I personally encountered, and one in the Word that

is promised prophetically that has not yet happened. I think they perfectly illustrate everything I have been trying to say.

I hope they bless you and encourage you to believe He will manifest His love for you just as supernaturally because He is never a respecter persons. He loves us all the same, and will meet our need for love just as supernaturally as He did for those in real life stories.

Listen with your heart and have faith to believe that your pain is not too great or your circumstances too hard for Perfect Love to cast out all your fear and give you joy starting today, as you ponder what love is surely ahead for you.

My Mother's Last Eight Days on this Earth

My Mother was saved, but didn't know the LORD intimately until right before she stepped into eternity with Him. **She was dying from a lifetime of unbelievable misogyny and hellish abuse that ultimately almost destroyed her, but Perfect Love!**

Very likely because of all the hellish abuse she had suffered since she was 14 from my father who was a Satanist and leader of a coven, and my step father who was the leader of a pedophile ring, her mind and body suffered and finally succumbed to 11 years of horrible Alzheimer's and Parkinson's Disease. It was so bad that she could not move or speak for the last 3 years of her life.

The nursing home called and told me that they expected her to die any moment, so I was rushing out the door as fast as I could. But Yeshua spoke to me and said, "Take your tape player and the CD with Mike Bickle praying through the Song of Songs with JoAnn McFatter singing in the background. Play it around the clock till she comes home with Me." I obeyed.

She lived eight more days, surrounded constantly around the clock by the Word of God, revealing her true identity that had never penetrated her battered body, soul or spirit before. Her bed was by a picture window, and with my help, Jesus started teaching her about His love for her as His Bride through a pair of doves who would light on the tree outside her bed. I would interpret what He was saying, like when one dove flew away from her mate, He said "I am **not like your husbands. You don't need to run from Me."**

Another time he said, "I don't want to take you. I want you to come voluntarily, because Love that is not voluntary is no love at all!"

I was sitting by her bed when she was ready to choose to be his bride with no more fear. The song was playing, "<u>Who is this coming up out of the wilderness, leaning on her Beloved?</u>"

Song of Songs 8:5-7

Listen:

"Who is this coming up from the wilderness leaning on her beloved?... Put me like a seal over your heart, like a seal on

your arm. For love is as strong as death... Many Waters cannot quench love, or rivers overflow it..."

<u>One moment I saw my mother's frail and broken body dying, and the next moment I saw a miracle!</u> She was totally restored, wearing her beautiful, long white wedding dress, arm in arm with Yeshua, her Bridegroom. They walked up into heaven together right in front of my eyes! I saw the most beautiful example of perfect love in action beyond what my human mind could ever have imagined! Only God's love could transform like that! And His love will be that glorious for her forever and ever forever! Hallelujah!

How could I cry? This was the most glorious moment of my whole life. I saw Perfect Love express true love for my precious mother who had only known hell with her husbands on earth. No more tears! No more Hell! I knew that she would only experience eternal love with her bridegroom forever! I felt only joy! That was the happiest day of my life.

I guess that is why the Song of Songs is my absolute favorite book in the Bible.

Revelation 22:17
"The Spirit and the Bride say, 'Come!'"

Until it is time and I experience my own personal miracle with my eternal, heavenly Bridegroom, this will be my constant cry for every human alive, no matter how hopeless their situation looks, how much pain they are experiencing or how late it seems!

Will you be ready when He comes for you? (It makes no difference if you are male or female. This intimate love relationship with God has nothing to do with sex — only intimacy and perfect love for every human.)

GOD'S REVELATION OF HIMSELF IS SURELY INFINITE

I Will Share One More Miraculous Account - The Destiny of Abraham's Entire Family

We See Nothing but Hellish Conflict Now, But God! One Promised Climax of Love on Earth: YHWH Elohim's Covenant Promises to Abraham and His Family:

Look with Me and Be Prepared to Be Shocked.

Let's Start with Hagar and Ishmael: She Encountered El Roi: The God Who Sees. *Genesis 16:1-13*

Understand that this name of God requires more explanation and anticipation relative to its fulfillment in the future. The context is sad and painful, involving the inevitable conflict between Sarai, Abraham's wife, and Hagar, her maid, that Sarai gave to Abraham in an attempt to figure a way to have a child without God. Be sure you hang with me to the end of the story. It is better than any Hollywood movie you will ever see!

The horror of being pregnant against her will, and the harsh treatment of Sarai caused Hagar to run away. In the seemingly impossible situation, Hagar meets the God who sees, El Roi in Hebrew, and hears His prophetic word about Ishmael, the son of Abraham, she is pregnant with. Hagar also receives prophetic hints toward future events that still have not happened yet, but they surely will.

Let me try to give you the punchlines that I hope will illustrate the love and justice of YHWH Elohim, that you may not yet have imagined! **Reading these passages certainly showed me that I need to read the back of the book (all of it, including the book of Revelation) before I think I understand the heart of YHWH Elohim and His prophetic justice that appears, even today, to be impossible! Get ready to be shocked as the plot thickens!**

Here are some of the things God revealed to Hagar, while Ishmael was still in the womb:

Genesis 16:10-16

- *"I will greatly multiply your descendants so that they will be too many to count."*
- *"You will bear a son; and you shall call his name Ishmael, because the LORD has given heed to your affliction. He will be a wild donkey of a man; his hand will be against everyone,*

- *and everyone's hand will be against him: and he will live to the east of all of his brothers."*

"Then she called the name of the LORD who spoke to her, 'You are El Roi (A God Who Sees)."

Then God Told Abraham About Covenant: The Difference Between His Relationship To Ishmael and Isaac.

Genesis 17:1-27

- *"I am God Almighty"*
- <u>*As for Me, behold, My covenant is with you; and you will be the father of a multitude of nations." "I will make you exceedingly fruitful, and I will make nations of you, and kings will come forth from you."*</u>
- <u>*"I will establish My covenant between me and you and your descendants after you throughout their generations for an everlasting covenant, to be God to you and to your descendants after you."*</u>
- <u>*I will give to you and to your descendants after you, the land of Canaan, for an everlasting possession; and I will be their God. Every male among you shall be circumcised."*</u>
- <u>*"... As for Sarai, your wife... I will bless her... I will give you a son by her, and she shall be a mother of nations; kings of people's will come from her."*</u>
- <u>*"And Abraham said to God, 'Oh, that Ishmael might live before you!' But God said, 'No.'"*</u>

- *But Sarah your wife... will bear you a son and you shall call his name, Isaac; and I will establish my covenant with him for an everlasting covenant for his descendants after him."*
- *"As for Ishmael, I have heard you; behold, I will bless him, and I will make him fruitful and will multiply him exceedingly. He shall become the father of 12 princes,*
- *And I will make him a great nation.*
- *But My covenant I will make with Isaac, whom Sarah will bear you at this season next year."*
- *Abraham, Ishmael, and all the men of their company were circumcised that day.*

But This Is Not the End of the Story

Get Ready to See God's Irrefutable Ways of Fulfilling Covenant Promises

There are centuries of conflict between the sons of Ishmael and the sons of Isaac and Jacob, and also the sons of Keturah, the wife of Abraham after Sarah's death. But listen to the Bible's promises for the destiny of Abraham's family. God's Word never comes back void.

Remember that Hagar, Ishmael's mother, was Egyptian. Ishmael was half Egyptian and the sons of Keturah are represented by the Assyrians! Abraham and Sarah were the father and mother of Israel, the covenant people of God. (God changed the name of Abram to Abraham and Sarai to Sarah when He made covenant with them.)

<u>Now listen to the rest of the family of Abraham's story. I'll bet you could not even imagine how it will turn out!</u>

Isaiah 19:18-25 NASB

- *<u>"In that day, five cities in the land of Egypt will be speaking the language of Canaan and swearing allegiance to the LORD of host"</u>*
- *<u>"In that day, there will be an altar to the LORD in the midst of the land of Egypt,</u> and a pillar to the LORD near its border. It will become a sign and a witness to the Lord of host in the land of Egypt, for they will cry to the LORD because of oppressors, and He will send them a Savior and a Champion, and He will deliver them."*
- *<u>Thus, the LORD will make himself known to Egypt, and the Egyptians will know the LORD in that day.</u>*
- *They will even worship with sacrifice and offering, and will make a vow to the LORD and perform. The LORD will strike Egypt, striking but healing, so they will return to the LORD, and He will respond to them and will heal them.*
- *<u>In that day, there will be a highway from Egypt to a Syria, and the Assyrians will come into Egypt and the Egyptians into Assyria, and the Egyptians will worship with the Assyrians."</u>*

(Assyria? Why Assyria? I had a hard time finding the connection of Abraham's family to the Assyrians, but finally found that **it is through his sons with Keturah after Sarah died. She was his second wife and the third woman** through which he had children, counting Hagar. <u>He had six more sons through Keturah to complete the promise of Yahweh that he would be the father of many nations!</u> The names of her sons were Zimran, Jokshan, Medan, Midian, Ishbak and Shuah.)

But wait a minute! What about Israel, the covenant people? Will they never keep covenant? Let's find out in Isaiah 19:24-25!

"In that day, Israel will be the third-party with Egypt and Assyria, a blessing in the midst of the earth, whom the LORD of Hosts has blessed, saying, 'Blessed is Egypt, my people, and Assyria, the work of My hands, and Israel My Inheritance.'"

Wow! Wow! Wow!

<u>What the LORD has done for me and so many others is awesome, but this restoration of Egypt, the people of Hagar and Ishmael and Assyria, the sons of Keturah before Israel comes into the kingdom of God, blows my mind! Finally, His covenant people, Israel bow down to their Savior, Yeshua (Jesus) to complete Abraham's family coming into the Kingdom of God.</u>

<u>In the end, Abraham's eternal family, as One, finally becomes sons of Abba Father forever. This victory and reconciliation through Father God, Yeshua, the Son and the Holy Spirit's perfect love is more than my finite mind can comprehend! No matter what they all do, He will keep covenant!</u>

If you are contemplating making covenant with YHWH Elohim, the one and only true God of agape love, don't forget the story! And never doubt that He will keep covenant with you, just like He did with Abraham!

OUR GOD (YHWH ELOHIM) IS TRULY AGAPE LOVE!

Only He could even imagine such restoration of a family! As the saying goes, "You can't make this stuff up!" Nobody would ever believe it. And only the blood of Jesus and the Power of Holy Spirit could ever make it happen! Shockingly, Israel, God's chosen people, are the last to come into the Kingdom of God, and surrender to belief in their Savior, Yeshua. (Jesus!) They will even go through the first half of the Tribulation, believing that the Antichrist is their Messiah! But our God will bring Abraham's whole family together in heaven in the end, including the Egyptians and the sons of Keturah, some of Israel's worst enemies! He is the true covenant keeper!

Oh Lord, do that for all of us and our families, please. Because of this awesome, true revelation of the future prophesied to us in Your Word, and because You are not a "respecter of persons," we can even believe for that kind of miracle from You, Perfect Love.

I bow down to worship the only true God, I am amazed by who He is and what He will do in the end! Hallelujah!

2

WHO AM I?

Let's lay the foundation for our understanding about our God-given identity through an awesome Gaither song sung by a precious and wise little girl:

You're Something Special[1]

"... God made you something special. You're the only one of your kind. He had a special purpose that He wanted you to find. So, He made you something special. You're the only one of your kind....

I have a little sister who's not at all like me. She can write a lovely poem, but I can climb a tree. My brother, too, is different with freckles on his nose. When my questions needed answered, He's the one who knows. My daddy mows the back yard. My

---

1.   "You're Something Special" by the Gaithers'

mommy makes the bed. My brother cleans his playroom. I see the dog gets fed.

And each one needs the other to help him through the day. And love must be the reason God planned it just that way.

That's why He made you special. You're the only one of your kind."

You are uniquely special, the only one exactly like you and an important part of the image and likeness of Creator God – important to Him and others. If you do not fulfill the complete destiny Father has for you, the world will never see His total image!

An infinite number of us have been created for this purpose. Amazingly, He has never run out of different DNA combinations because He is infinite in every way. Can you imagine how many humans it will take to manifest His entire image? So, He is still creating people in His image and likeness. But why would He want you and me? There is one reason – to have a real love relationship with us! His love is so big that it takes us all to fulfill His desire to express it!

So, Who Am I and Who Are You?

We Are All the Beloved of God
(Father, Son and Holy Spirit).

He Is Agape Love and We Are His Beloved –
Every Single One of Us.

In spite of our diversity, everyone has one core purpose and identity in common. We are all the Beloved of God. He is Perfect Love and we are created for a deep, intimate, voluntary agape love relationship with Him and each other. It is that core characteristic that makes us human.

As I said in the first chapter, His image can never be a programmed robot. He wants you and I to love and be loved as the primary reality and manifestation of our eternal lives.

Remember, our problem is that we each have the same choices that Adam and Eve had – free will. All humans are created with the freedom to love or not. Because of the fallen angels that went before us and rebelled against God, we have enemies like Satan and the harlot who are expert wicked deceivers. We have to choose whom we will believe, follow and obey. The consequences of our choices between true love and harlotry are either gloriously fulfilling or devastating beyond our most horrible nightmare.

Adam and Eve found this out the hard way. They were created to live in a perfect world with all of God's awesome creation, surrounded by perfect love forever. But their rebellion against original intent was disastrous for them and messed us all up big time.

Neither our bloodline, even if we go all the way back to Adam and Eve and their horrible choices, nor the individual circumstances of our birth influence His love. **We are all born by creation, not just biology, and there are no accidental creations. If you have felt shame or cursed by the circumstances of your birth or your bloodline, be healed from that lie. You weren't created by your par-**

ents,[2] but by God; and we were all created for love by the One who is Love.

Each of our life's story, the unique part of Jesus' body we function as, gifts from Holy Spirit and our life's message will be different because the part of His image we each are destined to portray will be as varied as He is infinite.

He revealed my life's assignment to me in a very dramatic and life-changing deliverance session many years ago. My understanding of the purpose of my life was never the same after that. Through this encounter, I knew the pattern my life would follow and the past and present battles started to make sense.

This passage also unveiled the shocking revelation that **our lives didn't begin on this earth! Our Creator God knew us before He put us here!** From Jeremiah, I learned that **this life on earth is a short-term assignment, a dot on an infinite line of eternal life! And we have a specific job to accomplish on this earth while we are here!** I had never heard anything like that. In case you are as clueless as I was, listen to the destiny word of God spoken in Jeremiah 1. Wow! This was Jeremiah's word, not mine, but Father God spoke to me very personally and prophetically through this word that day and I have never been the same since. I am not claiming in any way to be on par with Jeremiah's international prophetic call or anointing, but his call helped me hear mine. I hope that your reading this passage will

---

2. Jeremiah 1:5

help open a deeper understanding to you about your unique call and relationship to Father God.

Jeremiah 1:4-10 The Open Bible Expanded Edition

"Now the word of the LORD came to me saying, 'Before I formed you in the womb, I knew you, and before you were born, I consecrated you; I have appointed you a prophet.... Everywhere I send you, you shall go, and all that I command you, you shall speak. Do not be afraid of them, for I am with you to deliver you,' declares the LORD.

Then the LORD stretched out His hand and touched my mouth, and the LORD said to me, 'Behold, I have put My words in your mouth. See, I have appointed you this day ... to pluck up and break (pull) down, to destroy and overthrow, to build and plant.'"

As I type these words today, I can still feel the powerful call I felt all those years ago when He first spoke them to me! At that time, I was still in the church I had been raised in which did not even believe in women ministers, much less prophets. They believed that all the miraculous gifts like prophecy, healing and miracles had ceased and that women could not even teach men. A female teacher's call was only to teach children or other women.

And to complicate things further for me, trying to talk to my pastor, my prophetic gift is not conventional. I am a "plumbline prophet," responsible to line things up with the Word like a plumb-line lines up construction with right angles so the building is aligned properly and does not fall.

This call is to a watchman who sees or discerns the enemy coming or present before anyone else has a clue. He sees because God shows him supernaturally. Then he is held responsible by God to warn. In His Word, Father warns the watchman that if he or she does not warn that vulnerable person, his blood is on the watchman's hands.[3] Surely you can see why the watchman is never popular in any society. Some listen. Most don't. Rarely does anyone else see the enemy until it's too late. It requires faith in God to believe what you cannot see and most people don't walk in faith in God. Jeremiah is the perfect example of a watchman.

God even told Jeremiah, the powerful prophet to all of Israel and their enemies, that nobody would ever listen to him,[4] but he had to warn anyway. He had to watch Judah fall to Babylon for their harlotry against God and experience hellish abuse like being thrown in a pit for warning them. I am also very aware that most of the people I warn do not believe me or listen. It is not an easy call. All watchmen had better have the fear of God as one of their basic beliefs.

But that day I got set free for the first time to be who I am called to be, no matter the cost. I can't express the freedom I received or the price of great persecution this call has caused, especially while I was still in that denomination, trying to help them see the truth of Scripture. You can probably imagine. And I can imagine the price you pay, possibly in a very different way, to be who you really are in

---

3. Ezekiel 33:6
4. Jeremiah 7:27

the body of Christ. After all, **the same religious structure we fight today crucified our LORD for loving them perfectly!**

Do you understand what I am trying to express to you? As God was speaking to me through Jeremiah's experience, I was hearing God Himself tell me in His Word that the gifting I was experiencing really does legitimately exist. I cannot explain to you how freeing that was!

At that moment, for the first time, I was becoming free to be who I am created to be, no matter what anyone else says, believes or does. I never knew that who I was called to be existed until that day! My life changed because I started becoming me and am still becoming who He said I am. Did I warn wisely or with great maturity in the beginning? Of course not! At that point, I had no example except the Word and no mentor. Since that deliverance session, I dared to receive the anointing to at least warn about things my former church didn't even believe were issues.

Remember in the Introduction how I likened our journey together as a mining expedition, looking for treasures? It is crucial that we become the unique image of Him He created us to be, especially if our true identity and function in the body has been considered passed away or been covered up or called fake by evil religious spirits like I encountered. Go and look in the mirror. Now look again and say, **"I am a beautiful and valuable diamond in the rough, created to reflect the image of my God in a totally individual and important way like nobody else can."**

You Are Not Extinct!

The Holy Spirit's gift to the body of Christ you are called to manifest is still alive and well in the true church today! You are free to be who religion teaches is extinct! You are created to operate supernaturally by the power of Holy Spirit!

Keep seeing your true identity and let the Holy Spirit clean and polish you till you sparkle with His glory and you live amazingly supernaturally! **Every single one of us is created to manifest the supernatural gifts of Holy Spirit!**[5]

I learned that lesson the hard way and it took a long time. I don't want you to go through what I suffered. Trying to stay in the denomination I had been in all my life and honestly talking to my pastor about what I was learning in the Word made me the bull's eye of vicious religious spirits in the church. They stripped me of all the role I had previously been accepted to function in.

I was removed from singing in the choir, singing solos, teaching the college class in Sunday School and teaching ladies' Bible studies. My pastor even tried to get me fired from the Bible School where I had taught for years!

I'm a warrior, so I didn't give up. Instead, that abuse propelled me into searching for Kingdom movements with like-minded leaders. After years of searching, gifted Spirit-filled ministers helped me to get free and trained to continually go deeper. I am still very much in process. Freedom and spiritual growth is a life-long journey, mining for dia-

---

5. I Corinthians 12: 4-27

monds of truth. Let's all keep digging. Nobody has arrived at all truth except Jesus, but Holy Spirit of Truth is always eager to show us where to dig.

I hope that my testimony is helping free you to become who you are, no matter who tries to tell you differently. Father, please speak to each one reading my story and tell them who You created them to be. Then anoint them supernaturally to be that exact image of You that nobody else can ever manifest.

Maybe you are not saved yet because all you have seen is the religious structure I just described. If so, I am so sorry, because the true Creator God is nothing like that. He is Perfect Love and He died for you personally because He loves you more than He loves Himself. He proved that on the cross of calvary where He died for you.

Won't you become an important part of His and my family today? All you have to do is ask Him for a real life-changing encounter with Him that transforms your life and eternal destiny forever.

To be saved, you must believe that the Father God of Abraham, Isaac and Jacob of Israel is the Creator and only true God and Father of all mankind. And you must truly understand that His Son Jesus died on the cross to pay the price for the sins of us all, including yours. Salvation is not a head thing. The demons believe that way and shudder in fear! Salvation is a heart and spiritual encounter with God Himself. He has been waiting for you for a long time and He truly wants you to know Him and be with Him forever.

Once you are sure that you want to give your life to Him, you must confess and repent of your sins and trust that He will forgive, save and transform you to be like Him. Repentance means to turn around and walk the opposite way, not just say words.

As a public picture of your salvation and further act of faith, ask Him to lead you to the right person and Spirit-filled church to disciple you. You will need to be baptized in water and in the Holy Spirit. These acts of obedience will begin your transformation into an eternal, Spirit-filled new creation. And then you will forever be a member of the body of Christ.

Even though I don't know you, I feel excited at the thought of your becoming a part of my spiritual family. It's really important that you grow in your faith by getting in the Bible so God can reveal Himself to you. (I recommend the New American Standard Translation). As you grow and get to know your God, you can learn to hear Him speak to you and talk with Him intimately and regularly. Talking with God is called prayer, and it should be a two-way conversation. All of this is a process. But you can grow as close to Him as you want to, depending on the time you spend seeking Him. If you keep a daily journal of your conversations with Him, you will be amazed at the intimacy you will develop with Him quickly. Holy Spirit will love teaching you and training you to be who you are created to be. Also, pray for the right body of Christ to connect with that will help you grow. It's ok to visit a number till you find the one that you feel at home in.

Keep reading, as we will talk a lot more about the body of Christ and the supernatural life He created you for.

Beware of the Counterfeits
Major Error in Many Churches

How in the world did the church I was raised in and many others like them come to hate the Holy Spirit and His gifts and Spirit-filled believers?[6]

Let's go on a deep dig to uncover serious biblical errors in their theology caused by counterfeit infiltrators who are actually possessed or oppressed by wicked religious spirits determined to stagnate the growth of the church. They have convinced whole denominations that the gifts from Holy Spirit are extinct. **These evil spirits want to completely eliminate one third of God and treat Him like the enemy.**

We must each know who God created us to be – true Spirit-filled supernaturally gifted members of the body of Christ. We are all in His image, created by all three of the members of the God Head: God the Father, God the Son and God the Holy Spirit. First and foremost, we must re-

---

6. Let me tell you of the main reason I am familiar with – Freemasonry that has deliberately infiltrated the church. This organization is very occult and antichrist, as well as secretive and guilty of deceiving its own members of lower degrees about who they truly worship – Lucifer! Only the highest level of members are told the truth about their true beliefs and the meaning of their oaths and ceremonies. The Southern Baptist Church where I was raised is majorly infiltrated with this heresy.

member that God is love and His love in us is our greatest gift.

We Are Created to Eternally Be Part of God's Family

Let's take a few minutes to look at each member of the Trinity individually and our relationship with each One. I don't believe that the Church in general has done a very good job of encouraging us to seek out a personal relationship with each One. What is your experience? How do you see yourself and your relationship with Father, Jesus and Holy Spirit individually?

Father God's Children

The Bible uses word pictures to explain our identity and relationships with Him. Let's look at common experiences Father God desires to have with each one He creates.

Can you see yourself as a little child sitting in His huge lap together with other children?[7] Does this scenario allow you to feel perfectly loved and safe from any fear?

---

7. If you are truly struggling with picturing yourself in these very personal and intimate love relationships with God, inner healing and deliverance from your own individual childhood experiences and training may be necessary before you can totally know Him fully. Don't fear, but ask Him to set you free to know Him intimately and to show you who can help you. Keep pressing in to Him as intimately as you possibly can where you are right now. Never give up on intimacy with Him. If you have been abused, even in church, know that it was never Him. He alone is Perfect Love. It is time for you to be free and know Him more intimately than you have ever known anyone else.

His lap is infinitely huge. He could hold you and many other little children at one time - all equally accepted, loved, safe and free - red, yellow, black, brown and white, as one with nobody feeling out of place. How does this picture of the Family of God feel to you?

Then, growing up, can you see yourself as a son or daughter going to your Father God with any question or problem? Is He always present to cheer you on in every circumstance?

When it is time to pick a mate, would His counsel always be the most important and the same be true when picking a college and profession? At any age, should you know that His counsel and companionship as God is crucial above all others?

And when death is staring you in the face, because you know Him intimately, is there a need to fear? Or because eternity with Him is the joy that awaits you a split second later, will you be gloriously entering eternal life with Him?

Jesus' Bride

Seeing yourself as a child may not be hard for you, but understanding what it means for you to be the Bride of Christ Jesus may be difficult, especially if you are a man. This identity is certainly not homosexual or even sexual at all. It is totally about the most intimate spiritual relationship possible.

If we are truly saved because we have fully repented for our sins and given our whole lives to Him as our LORD, "we are now seated in the heavenly places in Christ Jesus"[8] at the right hand of Father God. Jesus now rules over all the earth and we do our part to rule with and in Him right now. We are organically and eternally connected to Him as members of His body. Each one of us has a different role in this process, just like different organs of the body work differently. But every single one of us is critically important to Him.

Even more amazing, we are the eternally perfectly loved Bride of Christ. He died for that! You may have had horrible experiences on earth in marriage.

Or you and your spouse may have had an awesome, beautiful, truly Christian marriage. In that case, you will both experience being a part of the corporate Bride of Christ. This is an intimate relationship like no other, far beyond human marriage.

The most intimate relationship possible becomes a reality when we experientially and eternally know and feel our true identity as the perfectly loved Bride of Christ. This intimacy is available for every believer right now and forever.

Holy Spirit Empowered and Gifted New Creations

Holy Spirit is the Gift and the source of our supernatural power. Do you know Him? Have you been baptized in Holy Spirit? When Jesus ascended into heaven, He told the dis-

---

8. Ephesians 2:6 NASB

ciples that He must go so Holy Spirit could come and give them power. He was talking about supernatural God power that only Holy Spirit can give us.

But they had to wait for God's perfect timing. God has His own timing, you know? Most people have no understanding that every year God has Appointed Times and associated Jewish Feasts with deep spiritual meanings.

Jews and many Christians from around the world go to Jerusalem to participate in these feasts. So God planned for the Holy Spirit to come with His power manifested through tongues of fire at that precise time and place in Jerusalem. He came as the fulfillment of the Jewish Feast of Pentecost.[9]

Because of God's synchronized timing,[10]Jewish believers and worshipers of YHWH Elohim from around the world were in Jerusalem on that holy day when Holy Spirit came. And they spoke many different languages.

He also made sure that when Holy Spirit fell on each believer and those waiting in the upper room spoke in tongues, everyone in earshot of the tongues could supernaturally hear the interpretation of those tongues in his

---

9. Robert Heidler does an awesome job of explaining the Jewish Feasts in the book *Messianic Church Arising. See p 184-189 for his discussion of The Feast of Pentecost. He teaches that there are three dimensions of Pentecost:*

1. Celebrating God's provisions; 2. Celebrating God's supernatural revelation through the Torah; 3. Celebrating the outpouring of Holy Spirit. Note that God times events in His calendar according to His feast and fast times He calls Appointed Times and Seasons.

10. Acts 2:37-41

own language! This was the sign that God had truly just manifested something totally new and supernatural that nobody had ever experienced before. This was God! Oh, there were mockers, as always, but those who had experienced it were forever changed.

Peter, for one, was obviously totally changed! He had just been transformed and anointed by Holy Spirit baptism. Can you imagine Peter, who had denied Jesus 3 times, now becoming the spokesman for the church to begin converting the very ones who had crucified His LORD?

He was now anointed and able to supernaturally explain what had just happened. He boldly confronted them for Jesus' crucifixion and preached the gospel without fear. He was now totally filled with new, supernatural Holy Spirit power and no more fear!

He was preaching as a new Spirit-filled creation, and his listeners from all different countries were "cut to the quick" with conviction by the Holy Spirit and saved! They had just been convicted that they had crucified their Savior, Father God's Son, and repentance was being granted to them.

It was this new baptism in the Holy Spirit that changed these close followers of Jesus into powerful evangelists. He had told them to wait for Holy Spirit power. And they had been obedient.

They had no idea what was going to happen. And they certainly had no expectation that they were about to be transformed into new bold creations never seen before.

How do you react to this historic event that totally changed the church? You can imagine how it affects me with my experience in the church I was raised in.

From this incredible beginning, Jesus' disciples went out emboldened and supernaturally equipped to win the world to Jesus as LORD and Savior of us all. And we can thank them and those they discipled for the Bible. They literally were empowered to willingly give their lives so we could know their LORD as ours.

In the Old Covenant, Holy Spirit came upon people to do miracles, but blood sacrifices were still required by Father. Jesus had not come to earth yet as their blood sacrifice, so they were still required to sacrifice bulls and goats as a prophetic picture of His sacrifice that was yet to come. But now Jesus had shed His blood for all mankind of all time and everything had totally changed. There was no more need for animal sacrifices.

That Old Covenant had become obsolete because Jesus had fulfilled it all. Now it was time for a completely New Covenant written by God for His new creation believers. Jesus had paid the price of sin in full for all mankind of all ages and had taken His place at the right hand of His Father to rule and reign with Him, awaiting His New Covenant as the God–Man to fully manifest. Everything had changed so much that a New Covenant was necessary to fully reverse the curse caused by Adam and Eve's rebellion.

The New Covenant
Jeremiah 31:31-33

"Behold, days are coming," declares the LORD, "when I will make a new covenant with the house of Israel and with the house of Judah, not like the covenant which I made with their fathers in the day I took them by the hand to bring them out of the land of Egypt, My covenant which they broke, although I was a husband to them," declares the LORD.

"But this is the covenant which I will make with the house of Israel after those days," declares the LORD, "I will put My law within them and on their heart I will write it; and I will be their God, and they shall be My people."

Now man, as new creations baptized in God the Holy Spirit, literally would be supernaturally part of the body of Christ, sitting at the right hand of Father God, empowered by His indwelling Holy Spirit, ruling and reigning in Christ Jesus.

This total transformation is what the baptism in Holy Spirit does. And that is why the enemy has determined to deceive everyone he can about the gifts that the indwelling and empowering Holy Spirit manifests in the New Testament, New Covenant body of Christ.

Just as we see in the book of Acts in the life of Peter, he had denied Jesus 3 times. But being baptized in the Holy Spirit transformed his life completely. Now he was a new creation with the supernatural power to stand up and boldly lead the same people he had been terrified of a short time ago to salvation – 3000 of them

<u>**that first day! Now that is supernatural power manifesting!**</u>

<u>**And this was only the beginning of New Testament Christianity that changed the whole world through these new creation believers we call Christians.**</u>

If we could have seen the big universal picture of what was happening, we would have seen the birth of the real Church, spiritually seated in Christ Jesus in the third heaven. Now men and women as new creations were ruling and reigning in the third heaven at the right hand of Father. In Christ, they were now each manifesting as eternal parts of Jesus' body. Holy Spirit was always the Gift and we each were created to manifest a part of His supernatural body and power in a specific, personal and unique way. They, through the baptism in the Holy Spirit, had become new creations. Anything less than or different from that is not the new covenant church!

I hope you see that Father, Jesus and Holy Spirit all three manifest their image and likeness in us to make up the total unique gift of who we are. Pretty supernaturally amazing, isn't it?

Who Are You and I and How Do We Relate?

And Exactly How Did They Become New Creations?

On Pentecost, Holy Spirit fell and the believers in Jesus were each baptized in Him with tongues of fire. At that moment, they were all transformed into a new creation

as a member of the body of Christ Jesus! Jesus' body, with Him as the Head, was taking its place at the right hand of Father God. This was the prize He had died for! This was the true church at that time, and it is still to grow with all who will choose to love and follow Him as their Savior and Bridegroom.

Everything had changed since Holy Spirit had come. That was why Jesus had told His disciples that He must go so Holy Spirit could come. Hallelujah!

For many years I had no real concept of the new creation and have never heard a sermon on the subject. I had taught that the ultimate victory plan for redeemed mankind is to take back what the devil stole from Adam and Eve. I thought that we were to return to ruling and reigning over the whole world like they did. We were forgiven and reinstated in dominion over the devil and all his demons because of the finished work of the cross of Jesus. Of course, we did this in Christ as His body sitting far above the devil who is under our feet.

I thought that was cutting edge theology because it was the best hope I had ever heard. The denomination I grew up in knew nothing about the Holy Spirit and His awesome part in New Testament Christianity. I never understood why Jesus told His disciples that He must go so Holy Spirit could come. I never saw this until God the Holy Spirit, my teacher, sovereignly showed me the new creation in the Bible. It had been there all along, but I never got it until I was writing this chapter! With that revelation, my whole concept of who I am got "born again!" I'm not just saved from my sins. I'm a totally new creation because I have been baptized in Holy Spirit!

Spiritually, I was blind about this glorious identity, but now I see! I had always thought that going back to where Adam and Eve left off and starting over was the ultimate hope for mankind. But now I know that our hope and reality as New Testament believers in Christ Jesus is light years beyond that! Here is what Holy Spirit, my teacher, has taught me:

Jesus (Yeshua) Is the One and Only 100% God-Man

Jesus came to Earth to empty Himself of His power as God and live as 100% man so He could legally die for us as a true man, pay the price for our sins and defeat Satan. His perfect blood sacrifice paid the debt in full that we could never pay.

Now He sits at the right hand of His Father as the perfect, victorious God-Man. He is 100% God and 100% Man. And He is now sitting far above all of creation. He has totally defeated the one who defeated Adam and Eve and robbed them of their God-given rulership over Earth.

But not only is He in that position ruling and reigning, totally in charge as King of Kings and LORD of Lords of all; there is more.

Jesus is not alone up there on His throne. He is not just an updated, better version of Adam. He is God and He is also The Perfect Man. He is the Head and every new covenant Christian is now a part of the body of our per-

fect resurrected Christ Jesus. We are now spiritually new creations in Him, ruling with Him.

We are not just new versions of Adam and Eve either! Nothing like us had ever existed before the finished work of the cross was completed by Jesus. But also, nothing like us ever existed until Jesus the God-Man went to His place in Heaven so that Holy Spirit could come upon man at Pentecost with power. That happened to those waiting in the upper room, as instructed by Jesus.

Holy Spirit came upon each one of them and they were baptized in Holy Spirit through His fiery tongues that were heard by everyone in earshot of those being Spirit baptized.

But those listening did not just hear the tongue itself, but the interpretation of Holy Spirit's message in tongues spoken to each of them in his own language. Many, many languages were translated supernaturally by Holy Spirit to set the stage for the salvation of those multitudes in Jerusalem for the Feast of Pentecost! This was the beginning of the world-wide New Testament Church! Wow! Have you ever thought of Pentecost or the new creation that way? I don't know about you, but I've been transformed through this Holy Spirit revelation! I had never seen tongues this way before.

Father, Jesus and Holy Spirit are One, not three separate

entities. **It took all three to make us new creations! Jesus paid our price as our sacrificial Lamb of God.**[11]

But Father had to rend the veil between us and Him. That kept mankind from dying in His presence in the Holy of Holies.[12]

Then **Jesus** had to go back to Heaven and take His place at the right hand of Father, ruling and reigning with Him.[13]

Jesus told His disciples that He had to go **so Holy Spirit** could come. He came to the Upper Room, baptizing them, manifesting as tongues of fire **to give them supernatural power necessary to be new creations.**[14] And He has never stopped giving of Himself to us so we can become New Testament new creations, too.

We are newly designed by Father to be the Body of Christ now ruling and reigning in Jesus as His body at the right hand of Father. After this whole process was completed, then and only then, old things had passed away and all things had become new!

We must look again and see this totally new creation that had never been seen before. Jesus our Savior is not sitting alone because He asked Father that we would be with Him. He bought us with His blood sacrifice of Himself. What a price! What love! I hope you are feeling it.

---

11. John 1:29 - 33; Revelation 12:11

12. Leviticus 16:1-34; Matthew 27:51; Mark 15:38; Luke 23:45

13. Mark 16:19

14. Acts 1:1-8

Now think about the seriousness of the huge rift in what we consider to be the true Christian Church. Let me ask you a question: Is it optional to God whether or not our "church" truly receives the Holy Spirit as the third part of His triune being (God the Father, God the Son and God the Holy Spirit)? Does He care if some Seminaries won't accept students until they sign a paper declaring that they do not believe in the baptism in the Holy Spirit?

Or is it optional to believe or disbelieve what Jesus said about Him needing to go to heaven so Holy Spirit could come to earth and fill believers in Jesus with Himself and His supernatural power? Let's look at what Jesus said about that issue before He went to Heaven:

Acts 1: 4-6

"Gathering them together, He <u>commanded</u> them not to leave Jerusalem, but to <u>wait for what the Father had promised,</u> 'Which,' He said, '<u>you have heard of from Me; for John bap-tized with water, but you will be baptized with the Holy Spirit and fire</u> not many days from now.'"

<u>Does this baptism in the Holy Spirit sound important to you, or just optional or even evil?</u> Is the baptism in the Holy Spirit the way a believer becomes a new creation seated in heavenly places in Christ Jesus as a legitimate part of the body of Christ ruling and reigning with Him? You decide what the Word of God says to you!

When we become new creations, He fills us with His love so that we who give all of our lives to Him uncondition-

ally are seated in Him as His body. We become a truly new creation, a totally new kind of being, never before seen.

We are not just seated with Him, but in Him as a part of His body. He is the Head and we are His body. We are one with our Beloved.

More of My Personal Story

Now let me continue with my personal story, hoping it will help you fully discover and fulfill your own destiny. Let me start at the beginning - in the delivery room:

I'm a warrior born on a battlefield, gasping for breath and fighting for my life because the panicking OBGYN nurse on call held Mother's legs together to keep me from being born before the doctor got there. The problem was that my head had already been born and she was choking me!

That was a clue for me that there is more than one super-natural power that has a plan for my life! **I experientially now know that each of us has both the awesome birth assignment from the one and only true God who created us, full of perfect love and an eternal destiny. But I was literally entering this world with a face-to-face en-counter with the other supernatural being who has a different plan for my life called the <u>"Satanic Birth As-signment."</u> When my head came out of the birth canal, Satan's birth assignment literally hit me in the face!**

In the last chapter, I told you a little about my mother's life – that she had two husbands. That means I had two fathers. <u>**My biological father was the satanist warlock leader of a coven and my step father was the leader of a pedophile ring**</u>. **That should give you a clue that my encounters with my Satanic Birth Assignment in the delivery room were only the beginning to a lifetime of intense warfare with high level demonic forces who have tried to make me their sacrifice all my life.** Before me, my father, the warlock, had sacrificed a number of other babies, and I was next on his list, but my mother fled from him right before I was born, saving my life. Praise God!

The fact that you are reading this book proves that YHWH had a higher, supernaturally protected birth assignment for me than Satan's plan to make me the sacrifice that my father was planning to give him more demonic power.

Father God saved my life and ultimately delivered me, but not before my father found me and put me through 7 years of satanic ritual abuse and programming! Then he moved out of town, probably running from the Law. But my mother then married my pedophile step-father. He put me through another 5 years of pedophilia through his ring of bisexual "friends." I had to live in the house with him and his wickedness until I married at 21, when I was in Graduate School. Understand that a victim of Satanic Ritual Abuse and Pedophilia is ritually programmed, so you are living a totally dissociated life and have no idea what is going on, sometimes for many years. You are living at least two lives and don't know it! In His great mercy, God often doesn't let the victim know his or her history until many years later - until there is a support team who can help with deliverance and inner healing. All the years of hell, I was truly saved and very involved in church (Not the one I have been talking about. This was much earlier.) I was a trained deliverance minister for years before I remembered anything of my own ritual hell!

Ultimately, Father God led me on an awesome path of deliverance and inner healing that included a Masters and Doctorate Degree in Practical Ministry with concentrations in Prophecy, Deliverance, Spiritual Warfare, Counseling and Christian Living. What a breath of fresh truth! What freedom!

That journey has trained and enabled me to walk out my destiny and help others get and stay free from Satan's plans to destroy them. Praise God for deliverance that is available for all of us. He makes sure we have a chance to choose the path to eternal life and the perfect love Jesus died to give each and every one of us.

That very real war between the Kingdom of Heaven and the Kingdom of Hell for our eternal destiny is largely unseen or ignored, even by most churches. We will not choose that path of deception on our treasure hunt, right? From personal experience, I can tell you that there is nothing but hell itself along that road of denial and spiritual "La -La Land." Let's move on into the light of the One who is the Light of the World. His name is Yeshua (Jesus).

Everyone's life is like a good book that is continually being written until we take our last breath – a cliff hanging mystery until the end. Until then, nobody but God knows if it will be a terrible Greek tragedy or a beautiful love story. Why? This is primarily because of one of

two reasons. The most common reason is that free will thing we have talked about - free will to choose who we want to follow – Abba Father or Satan. But our issue is that we are often not even warned that we are responsible to choose which one it will be! And we often are so young and naïve or so brainwashed by wicked people and deceivers where we least suspect them to be that we are clueless. Our school teachers or even our relatives often are the most dangerous abusers. Tragically, most churches today are absolutely clueless or worse! And many, like my church I told you about, are much worse because they have been taken over by Luciferian Masons! What I experienced was even worse than that, involving satanic ritual abuse, sacrificing children to Satan and programming children, involving creating split personalities through trauma so horrible that it causes dissociation that can only be dealt with by someone well trained through high level deliverance specialists who understand SRA and know their LORD Jesus well.

To the uninformed, it might seem like the choice between a true Christian lifestyle and satanism should be a no-brainer, but it definitely is not! This is a more serious problem than ever now that truth is censored and labeled conspiracy theories. And blatant lies define mainstream media and the curriculum of the schools. Nobody is born seeing all the hidden dimensions of evil in his world. Much is disguised by supernatural enemies who make sure we are deliberately dumbed down and even brainwashed and programmed. If a church or denomination teaches that Holy Spirit and His supernatural gifts are to be banned from the church, you have definitely met someone who is terribly deceived or worse!

Later, we may wake up and see how enemies have infiltrated every aspect of our lives and world. By this time, we may have seemingly messed up our destiny beyond hope. But YHWH's plan is infinitely more brilliant and powerful than our self-destructive strategies or even Satan's best laid schemes to destroy us.

We still may have no understanding of generational curses, supernatural plots or even the very complex dynamics in our own family line. We usually think that our care givers and relatives, whoever they are, are safe. That can be good or bad, depending on which supernatural powers they are ruled by. Regardless of reality, we enter this battle like I did, as innocent, helpless babies beginning our journey in the real fallen world.

My whole story would take volumes that most people could not handle reading, so I will deliberately leave out a lot, but let me just say that I thank God for dissociation! This is a major way our Father helps people with backgrounds like mine survive their trauma.

I believe that there are many horror stories about my life that I will never remember because it is not necessary to relive hell to be free. For example, when I was about 11, we lived in a house that I have no memories of at all except for the bed I was tied hand and foot in, blindfolded and gagged so I could be sexually abused by my step father and his homosexual pedophile "friends."

I've had a few deliverance memories relative to that place, but in general, I remember only critical satanic rituals during grade school.

My "normal" memories begin when I went to Junior High, after I threatened my step-father and he stopped the abuse! (Understand that I didn't remember any of this until many years later!)

Perfect Love can deliver me some other supernatural way besides having to relive all the hell! He allows me to experience deliverance from captivity of dissociated parts still in places of captivity when I am ready to face the hell.

I trust Him to be Perfect Love. He will not torture me with unnecessary memories nor withhold truth I need to know. He is the only one who knows my whole story. And He is supernaturally capable of totally healing me from horrors beyond my human ability to survive without going crazy! He truly is Perfect Love.

In contrast, I don't ever remember a time when God wasn't there! I know that this is hard to believe or understand if you have never experienced dissociation, but it is very true! It's like I have always known Him, yet I vividly remember my salvation experience!

I had been a deliverance minister for many years when I began having memories of my own abuse!

His timing is perfect and He usually waits until you have someone who has some understanding of what you are going through before the memories are released into your conscious mind.

Eventually, when I could handle it, I went through many years of extensive inner healing, deliverance, training, a Masters and Doctoral degree and lots of experience so I could get free and help others. Our God who is perfect Love also has perfect timing for His destiny to walk out for each one of us! And the process of healing and learning experience never stops until He takes us home.

Back to our original questions: In the beginning, we certainly have no clue that we have two opposing kingdoms vying for our eternal lives. We don't know that God and our enemies have diametrically opposite birth assignments planned to influence our every decision. We have no idea about the eternal danger of certain turns we almost took. Or more tragically, maybe we do know all too well that we took the wrong turn way back there.

But listen closely! If you are still breathing, it is not too late to repent and make an about face! The God of Perfect Love is right there to receive you in His arms. Repent, if you have made major wrong turns. He will show you how to turn around and begin your walk toward deliverance, freedom and His perfect love. It's not too late.

Everyone has to exercise free will and face the consequences. We will either choose the road to eternal life with God who is love or the road to eternity in hell with Satan, his fallen angels and demons.

Do you realize that Satan does not only hate God and continually try to overcome Him and destroy His family corporately? He also hates each of us personally because we each present a unique threat to him. Father God is not surprised or freaked out by him. The victory of His Son on the cross has insured the victory of every one of us if we will bow our knee to Him. He promises that He can work all things together for our good. And He always will for all those who love Him and are walking out His purposes in their lives. (Romans 8:28)

Romans 8:37-39 Amplified Version
***"...in all these things we are more than conquerors." and gain an overwhelming victory through Him who loved us* (so much that He died for us.)**

Paul's word for conquerors means more than winning the war. It also means carrying away all the spoils from your personal enemy. That is what your treasure book, the Bible, says about who you are and what you are created to be and do. Feel better? Ready to fight to win big and take back all your enemy stole? I am. Let's go.

So how do you fit into this story? Do you really know who you are and have you received Holy Spirit power that Jesus died to give you? What treasures do you have hidden in you that you may not have even mined yet? Have you experienced the LORD's glorious eternal love story? No matter how badly you might have blown it in your mind, have you given God a chance to transform you into the new creation He created you to be so you can become the full image of God you were created to be?

God is love and we each have forever to be loved perfectly. It is never too late, as long as you are still alive. Even today could be your day to be transformed like Peter. You might have a hard time believing me because of lies about you that you have believed. Listen carefully to the truth.

No creation by God is ever an accident, irrelevant, unimportant or unloved. It takes every one of us to reflect the total image and likeness of God and we won't truly see his total image unless we see Him in everyone. That includes you, no matter if anyone else ever sees who you really are. He does and will forever love you.

You are essential to the complete picture of the image and likeness of God, so now let's dig deeper as we mine for our hidden identity, probably in the form of a huge diamond in the rough! We don't want anyone to miss your multifaceted reflections of His light!

The Bible uses word pictures to teach us who we are and how we are to relate to one another and Him. Let's look at what the Word says and see if we can figure out how we fit in each word picture. Let me assure you that you do fit and whichever word picture drawn in **your treasure book won't be complete without you! Everyone is essential and there are no misfits.**

Who Are You, Ultimately and Forever?

You Are Created to Eternally Be the Bride of Christ.

The Final New Wineskin Is the Spirit and the Bride.

Back to my story, past present and future: **as I have told you, my biological father was a satanist, so my Satanic**

Birth Assignment was to be a sacrifice. That was the reason for my birth experience and a whole lot more that was ahead for me.

But God! Perfect Love came down from Heaven and snatched me out of danger! The doctor got there and I was born and not choked to death, but certainly traumatized.

Next, I found myself in a warm incubator, saved from my enemy. This close call with destruction scenario has become a very familiar theme for me in many arenas, but I have learned to trust in my Savior to always show up, often seemingly at the last minute and snatch me from hell's plan. These close calls always prove to me who I am to Him. I am not primarily just a warrior in danger of annihilation. I am His Beloved! And so are you and everyone else He ever created. Many just don't know it yet.

I just experienced one of those special, miraculous moments this morning. My blood pressure had been at stroke level for over a week – 178 – and I was getting scared. I had cried out and He answered, "You are dying of a broken heart and I do not want you to die!"

So last night I pressed in to seek Him as my Bridegroom, reading Song of Songs in the Passion Translation until nothing else mattered but Him. He took me to the place that I was in tears over His love for me and I knew that whatever happens in the nation or my life, it doesn't matter. I do not need to be afraid of anything. I will finish the time He has assigned for me to be here on earth and then I will be with Him forever.

This morning my blood pressure has gone down 38 points! Glory to my Healer and Bridegroom!

Let me share excerpts from what He said to me last night. This is as much for you as it is for me. He loves us all perfectly. **His words are the reason my heart was healed last night.**

Song of Songs 2:10-14

"Arise...hurry... Come away with me! The season has changed. The bondage of your barren winter has ended, and the season of hiding is over and gone....

Can you not discern this new day of destiny breaking forth around you? The early signs of my purposes and plans are bursting forth. The budding vines of new life are now blooming everywhere ... There is change in the air ....

Arise ... and run with me to the higher place, for now is the time to arise and come away with me. It was I who took you and hid you up high in the secret stairway of the sky."

He couldn't have chosen a more intimate passage to draw me into. I live at Beth El, like the original Beth El, Israel, where my Grandfather Jacob saw the stairway to heaven and angels going up and down a Gateway to Heaven, House of God. What a personal invitation for My Healer to use to heal me. He is not a respecter of persons. He will set you up with your perfect divine appointment for healing, too.

Let me share another divine appointment, many years ago. At the perfect time when Father knew that I was about to face one of Satan's most wickedly and cleverly attempted death blows, a man of God showed up in my life. He is a "man's man," who grew up with some of the toughest, most masculine guys you could imagine. Jesus had encountered him in an incredible way and taken him deeper than I had ever seen, into an intimate, experiential revelation and relationship with Him.

He knew Him in a way I had never even heard of – as his Bridegroom. What? A tough guy's Bridegroom? That was hard to imagine, but definitely real to him. He had my attention, so I kept listening. It was very obvious that he was not homosexual or effeminate in any way – quite the opposite. I think Father used him deliberately and specifically to teach me and thousands of others that Jesus' love for His bride is not sexual at all, but deeply intimate. He made it obvious that the bridal identity for the believer is not just for women, but it is the ultimate mature biblical relationship of love planned by Father God for everyone who loves Him.

This core identity for me is the reason I am still alive and the reason, in spite of all sorts of demonic attacks, life-threatening sicknesses, betrayals and times I was tempted to give up and even once prayed to die, I'm still His Warrior Bride. And that is why that is the name of my ministry.

I hope you, male or female, will come to know who you are in this most intimate way possible. Knowing Father's love is crucial, beautiful, safe and essential for every human.

There is nothing that will ever replace it. But bridal love of man or woman with Jesus is the ultimate of intimacy.

In the end when Jesus has to go through the unbelievable betrayal of most people He died for, it will be the corporate Bride, male and female, who will never leave His side. In His darkest hours, probably not too far in the future, we are created to make sure He is never alone. We must not forget that He has always been there for us when we were alone and being betrayed. He is continually filling us with His perfect love so we receive His love to give to others, even to those who have hurt us most deeply. What a gift!

Here is another nugget in Revelation 22, the very culmination of the whole Bible. If you were asked who would join Holy Spirit, representing the true body of Christ, who would give the last call, the final chance to choose eternal life and escape eternal hell, who would you expect God to choose as His human spokesmen?

Perhaps you would say the apostles and prophets or the whole five-fold ministry leaders. Actually, apostle or not, the final crucial identity of the mature believer who speaks as one with Holy Spirit for Father and Jesus in the last call is the corporate Bride! In the Ephesians 4 passage about the five-fold ministry, there is an "until". Many of you are probably five-fold ministers, as I am, but we do not stop growing in maturity and intimacy with that identity. We are still growing. In the final chapter of the Bible, we all are to mature to the identity of the corporate Bride, pictured by the New Jerusalem, the Final New Wineskin of believers in the end.

If you have never stepped into this level of intimacy, won't you come now, so you can be part of that final call?

**If Holy Spirit is Convicting You
That You Need to be Baptized
in His Holy Spirit,
All You Have to do is Ask Jesus
to Baptize You in Holy Spirit,
and He Will.**

Jesus lived as a man, died and rose again, and even went into Hades[15] to take captivity captive, motivated by His love for His Bride. Now His desire is that we will forever be with Him throughout eternity.

My friends, receive His Perfect Love for yourselves, because He would have done it all just for you, even if you had been the only one alive! That is what He said to me when I was saved at 12.

I will never be the same because I now know and accept the reality that I am not my old man with all my weaknesses.

I am in Christ, the God-Man. He alone is my Head and I am a crucial part of His body. I am seated far above all

---

15.   Hades is Greek, the equivalent of Sheol in Hebrew. The dead are held here till judgment. This is not Hell, which is Gehenna, seen as the lake of fire. In a vision John sees the sea, death and Hades give up their dead and each person is judged according to what he has done, and if he is guilty, he is thrown into Hell depicted by the lake of fire, where the wicked are judged. (simplybible.com).

our enemies, ruling and reigning with Him. He paid the price to make all that a reality.

In Him I cannot lose a battle because He never has or will. All who are truly new creations as a part of His body are seated far above all in the Third Heaven. We are completely and forever safe, where every enemy is under our feet.

Our Biblical Treasure Book says it this way:

II Corinthians 5:17
"... if anyone is in Christ, he is a new creation; the old things passed away; behold, new things have come."

3

WHY AM I HERE?

As I pondered this huge question, the Lord answered me by saying that you can't know why you are here unless you know what time it is! We are here for "such a time as this." Our time on earth is very related to what He is doing right now, and, apparently, He wants to tell us what that is!

He has my attention. How about you? This is what I am hearing Him reveal to us:

"The Church Age is almost over and the time for the rapture of My church is rapidly approaching. **You are not destined for wrath,**[1] *and My wrath on this earth against My enemies who have refused to repent of their iniquities against Me and receive My mercy is coming, as described in the Book of Revelation.*

------

1. I Thessalonians 5:9-10 NASB **"For God has not destined us for wrath,** but for obtaining salvation through our Lord Jesus Christ, who died for us."

There has never been a time like this on the earth before! Press in to hear Me and obey me very carefully because I love you and want you to be prepared as I do things nobody has ever seen before! **You were born for such a time as this** *- you and everyone else on the earth now!"*

Wow! Speak, LORD, your servant is listening.

His answer shifted me into an in-depth study of the rapture (Latin for "catching away"), the second coming of Jesus, and even the whole Book of Revelation. Not that I have become an expert, but I do know a lot more than I learned even from my Masters and Doctorate degrees that I so enjoyed learning from. God's Word is infinite in His revelation and I have an expectation that Holy Spirit is about to take us deeper than we have ever been before on these controversial subjects. Also, He is warning us that we have never been at such a critical time before! Ready for a deep dig, Miners?

Critical Questions about End Time Biblical Revelation

The Rapture and the Second Coming

- What does the Bible say about the rapture (catching away)?
- Is the Second Coming of Jesus the same time as the rapture or a different time?
- What do the books of I and II Thessalonians, I Corinthians and Revelation say about these end times issues?

- In light of all this, why are you and I here now and not earlier or later?
- Lord, I know that You never waste time or give us busy work to do, so I am taking this assignment very seriously and cry out for deep revelation and application for me and all who read this book, either before or after the rapture!

The Rapture (Catching Away)

There is so much controversy about the rapture, so let's be very careful to let the Word speak for itself and allow every reader to decide what he or she believes based on the Word itself and not anyone's interpretation, except Holy Spirit's.

I Corinthians 15:50-55 NASB

"Now I say this, brethren, that flesh and blood cannot inherit the kingdom of God, nor does the perishable inherit the imperishable. Behold, I tell you a mystery; <u>we shall not all sleep, but we shall be changed in a moment, in the twinkling of an eye, at the last trumpet, for the trumpet will sound, and the dead will be raised imperishable, and we shall be changed. For this perishable must put on the imperishable, and this mortal must put on immortality, then will come about the saying that is written, 'Death IS SWALLOWED UP in victory. O DEATH, WHERE IS YOUR STING?'"</u>

Wow! This short passage is loaded with strange revelation! What does it mean that not all die and death is swallowed up in victory and has no sting? It says that this all happens in a moment, **at the last trumpet,** and we are changed into something imperishable. **He did warn that this event is a mystery, and it certainly is - a mystery we call the rapture.**

In trying to exegete the biblical passages about the rapture, this **last trumpet reference** was one of the most difficult for me to understand, combined with the statement about the **wrath of God.**

I spent a lot of time reading and re-reading the Scripture and getting nowhere, but God! He finally led me on line to a wonderful discovery: **versebyverseministry.org. Hallelujah!**

They put everything in the <u>right historical timeframe</u> through their understanding of the <u>Jewish Feasts</u> so that it makes perfect sense now. I was so grateful!

Here is the explanation: the issue is timing. Paul was writing to the Corinthians, but John was writing to all of us through the Book of Revelation 40 years later! There is no way that Paul's audience would have known anything about the judgments of God's wrath against the evil ones. These were recorded by John in the Book of Revelation that had not been written yet.

But they were all very familiar with the <u>Jewish Fall Feast of Trumpets and celebrated these Fall Feasts every year. The Feast of Trumpets ends with a great trumpet blast</u>.

Many believe that this last trumpet timeframe may very well picture the <u>rapture of the church happening during</u>

the Fall Feasts. The Bible says that we will not know the day or hour, but this could be a hint about the Jewish Biblical Season when the rapture happens.

<u>**This timing before the wrath starts would put the rapture Pre-Tribulation. And we who are born again believers in Jesus would miss all the wrath of God that happens during the Tribulation time of the Antichrist. Hallelujah!**</u>

I understand that the Bible is telling us that whatever the Word records as **wrath is not our destiny if we are believers.** The word translated "wrath" is #3709 in Strongs Concordance and has meanings that truly show the long-suffering heart and yet totally just character of our LORD. He is both Ancient of Days, the ultimately Just Judge, but also Perfect Love. He is also both our Father and our Bridegroom, who created us to spend eternity in perfect love relationships with Him in a perfect family. We are destined to have nothing bad between us, ever, throughout eternity. And He is also Holy Spirit with limitless power so that He can keep every promise to us.

Wrath means "divine judgment inflicted upon the wicked." We can see just from this definition that God would never inflict wrath on anyone but His greatest enemies. This fact should also tell us that the rapture when He removes the true church from this earth will come before the time of Tribulation wrath starts.

But on the flip side of these facts is the reality that **wicked enemies of God and man will not spend eternity with the family of God.** Our just God must both judge and eternally punish His enemies who would not repent and accept Jesus' death on the cross as payment for their sins and worship Him as their Lord. It is these wicked people who will suffer the wrath of God during the Tribulation and forever. **Wrath is only for those who have missed their last chance to repent for their wickedness** and turn to the LORD who is Perfect Love, even if it happens at the last second like the thief on the cross hanging beside Jesus.

It is from this wrath that true believers are spared.

I Thessalonians 4:13-18 NASB

The Rapture
The Believers of Paul's Day
Were Worried about
The Eternal Destiny of Their Loved Ones
Who Had Gone on before Them,
So Paul Informed Them:

"...We do not want you to be uninformed, brethren, about those who are asleep, that you may not grieve, as do the rest who have no hope. For if we believe that Jesus died and rose again, even so **God will bring with Him those who have fallen asleep in Jesus.** *For this we say to you by the word of the Lord, that we who are alive, and remain until the coming of the Lord, shall not precede those who have fallen asleep.* **For the Lord Himself will ascend from heaven with a shout, with the voice of the archangel, and with the trumpet of God; and the <u>dead in Christ shall rise first.</u>** <u>**Then we who are alive and remain shall be caught up together with them in the clouds to meet them in the air, and thus we**</u>

shall always be with the Lord. Therefore, comfort one another with these words."

I Thessalonians 5:9-11 NASB

*"For **God has not destined us for wrath**, but for obtaining salvation through our Lord Jesus Christ who died for us, that whether we are awake or asleep, we may live together with Him. **Therefore, encourage one another, and build up one another ...."***

Having repeatedly read the Book of Revelation, which is full of the wrath of God, I find the Pre-trib rapture theology to make biblical sense. To me, this statement says that <u>true believers will be gone before the wrath of God against God's enemies begins in the Book of Revelation. The Church Age will be over and the true church will be raptured before the Tribulation, which is full of God's wrath against the Antichrist and his followers. We are not destined for the wrath of God</u> against His enemies. After looking at these Scriptures again with the understanding of the Fall Feasts, these passages make sense to me as revelation for a pre-tribulation rapture of the true church. After Revelation 3, the church age is over, and we are gone! The last of that chapter says, "He who has an ear, let him hear what the Spirit says to the churches." What do you hear?

I Thessalonians 5:23-24

"Now may the God of Peace Himself sanctify you entirely; and may your spirit and soul and body be preserved, completely

without blame at the coming of our Lord Jesus Christ. Faithful is He who calls you, and He also will bring it to pass."

The Second Coming of Jesus

Matthew 24:20-31 NASB

"But <u>immediately after the tribulation</u> of those days. THE SUN WILL BE DARKENED AND THE MOON WILL NOT GIVE ITS LIGHT, AND THE STARS WIL FALL from the sky, and the powers of the <u>heavens will be shaken</u>."

"<u>And then the sign of the Son of Man will appear in the sky; and then all the tribes of the earth will mourn, and they will see the SON OF MAN COMING with power and great glory</u>."

"And He will send forth His angels with a GREAT TRUMPET and <u>THEY WILL GATHER TOGETHER His elect from the four winds, from one end of the sky to the other</u>."

Let me point out some **logistics** of these passages we have looked at that are very relevant to the subject of whether the catching away or rapture and the Second Coming are two separate or the same events. Look and listen carefully.

In the 1 Thessalonians passage, the LORD descends from heaven with a shout, the voice of the archangel and trump of God. The <u>dead in Christ rise first</u> and meet Him in the air.

Then <u>those believers who are alive and remain (on earth) are caught up (raptured) to meet Him in the air.</u> And they will <u>ever</u> be with Him.

In the second passage of Matthew 24, there are completely different logistics. First, the Word gives us very different timing - immediately after the Tribulation. Much as happened during the seven year Tribulation, especially wrath, which is mentioned thirteen times!

I believe the true church has already met Jesus in the air. They have been with Him for those seven years, instead of the suffering under the hand of the Antichrist during the Tribulation.

So, the Bible is talking about a different group of people from those who went up in the Rapture. These people, who are still on Earth during the Tribulation, have missed the Rapture, because they were not Pre-Tribulation believers.

They have already suffered through the first six seals of the Tribulation, including the arrival of the Antichrist, war, famine, Death, and Hades that kill over one fourth of the earth with the sword, famine, pestilence, and wild beasts, martyrs, and hellish disasters that terrorized everyone so badly. Because of this, they hid themselves from the wrath of the Lamb.[2]

They are about to experience the seventh seal of their judgments, called Trumpets, but their chance to be saved has not passed because of the great grace of our

---

2. Revelation 6:1-17: "... Fall on us and hide us from the presence of Him who sits on the throne, and from the wrath of the Lamb; for the great day of their wrath has come: and who is able to stand?"

<u>God. More souls from every tribe, tongue, people and nation are saved after the Rapture than you can count.</u>[3]

Why would they truly change so much that they would now become true believers? The reasons obviously will vary, but think of what they have been through and how their mindsets about themselves and their relationship with God may have changed. Consider these factors:

- The shock of the Rapture, especially if they thought they were saved, but they didn't go.
- All children disappearing,
- The severity of God's judgments that they have already lived through,
- Re-evaluating their total eternal relationship with Jesus.

What Happened to The Truly Repentant People?

Revelation 7:9-17

"After these things I looked, and behold, a great multitude which no one could count, from every nation and all the tribes, peoples, and languages, standing before the throne and before the Lamb, clothed in white robes, and palm branches were in their hands;

---

3. Revelation 7:1-17: Because of His great mercy and grace, our great God shows mercy. He seals and protects the 144,000 Jewish bondservants from every tribe, and the great multitude, more than you can count, from every nation, tribe, people, and tongue. Oh, how we thank You for Your great mercy and grace!

and they cried out with a loud voice, saying, 'Salvation belongs to our God who sits on the throne, and to the Lamb.'"

And all the angels were standing around the throne and around the elders and the four living creatures; and they fell on their faces before the throne and worshiped God, saying,

'Amen, blessing, glory, wisdom, thanksgiving, honor, power, and might belong to our God forever and ever. Amen.'

Then one of the elders responded, saying to me, 'These who are clothed in the white robes, who are they, and where have they come from?' I said to him, "My lord, you know." And he said to me, 'These are the ones who come out of the great tribulation, and they have washed their robes and made them white in the blood of the Lamb. For this reason they are before the throne of God, and they serve Him day and night in His temple; and He who sits on the throne will spread His tabernacle over them. They will no longer hunger nor thirst, nor will the sun beat down on them, nor any scorching heat; for the Lamb in the center of the throne will be their shepherd, and will guide them to springs of the water of life; and God will wipe every tear from their eyes.'

Hallelujah for the grace of God and His forgiveness, even at the last moments of time to repent and be eternally saved from judgment."

Then He gathers His people, who were raptured, now not from the Earth, but from the sky where they were taken up to during the Rapture seven years earlier.

We must consider a number of different groups of people in these passages: the true church that has al-

ready been raptured pre-tribulation, the innumerable harvest throughout the whole world who are saved by grace during the Tribulation, the unbelievers who have been left behind and continue to rebel agains the true God and never get saved, and Israel.

Remember that Israel believed that the Antichrist was their Messiah until he went into the Temple and declared himself to be God, mid-tribulation. Then what happened to them? Let's look it up in the Bible.

Matthew 24:15-25:46 NASB

Jesus warns His disciples in great detail about the perilous times ahead for all mankind. He uses word pictures that are graphic and critical to our understanding of the times we live in, hundreds of years later. We must take these warnings very seriously, as Israel should.

Obviously, they haven't, and will end up following their worst enemy, the Antichrist. By mid-tribulation, they will wake up with what the Bible calls the Abomination of Desolation. Let's listen to Jesus' warning in His Word to His people, Israel. They will wake up mid-tribulation, to how they have been deceived by the Antichrist, as Jesus was directing them in Matthew so long ago:

" ... when you see the ABOMINATION OF DESOLATION *which was spoken of through Daniel the prophet, standing in the holy place—let the reader understand—then those who are in Judea must flee to the mountains. Whoever is on the housetop must not go down to get things out of his house. And whoever*

is in the field must not turn back to get his cloak. But woe to those women who are pregnant, and to those who are nursing babies in those days! Moreover, pray that when you flee, it will not be in the winter, or on a Sabbath. For then there will be a great tribulation, such as has not occurred since the beginning of the world until now, nor ever will again. And if those days had not been cut short.

... False Christ's and false prophets will arise and will provide great signs and wonders, so as to mislead, if possible, even the elect.

... Do not believe them. For just as the lightening ... flashes ... so shall the coming of the Son of Man be ... "

The Jews will flee from the Antichrist in horror. I have found it difficult to find the biblical details I would like to find about the time between this mid-tribulation even and the end of the Tribulation, but I will share what I have discovered momentarily.

At the end of this seven-year reign of Antichrist called the Tribulation, the sun darkens, the moon does not give its light and stars fall.

<u>Then the sign of the Son of Man appears in the sky (not on earth)</u>. Finally, the people of all the tribes on earth see who Jesus truly is and mourn! Horrified, they see the Son of Man coming on clouds with power and great glory and realize the reality of their deadly deception.

Jesus comes, appearing, along with angels from one end of the sky to the other, and the sound of the trumpet, and clouds of great glory, that includes the great cloud of witnesses.

<u>These passages prove that the Rapture and the Second Coming are definitely two different events. The people of God are already in the air, where He has gathered them from one end of the sky to the other. They are no longer on earth or destined for wrath.</u>

<u>Therefore, the Rapture and Jesus' Second Coming are two separate events at two different times.</u>

What Happens to the Jews?

Romans 11 NASB

We left them running from the Antichrist, mid-tribulation, after being horrified when he entered the temple and declared himself to be God. They realized how deceived they had been and were running for their lives. Do they get wiped out by the Antichrist? Do they ever find their Messiah? What happens during the last three and a half years of the Tribulation? Do they all end up in hell, or do they ever believe in Jesus as their Messiah? History is not over yet, but we can learn from the Bible what to expect, even though sometimes, like now, we have to dig even more deeply to find our treasures. Right, miners?

Let's look at Romans 11. I find that passage very enlightening about how God sees His Chosen People and His power to save.

"I say then, 'God has not rejected His people, has He?' ... His people He foreknew ..."

Paul goes on to quote Elijah crying out to God for himself against Israel, believing that he is the only prophet left in Israel. God shocked him with His answer that He has 7,000 others who had not bowed to Baal. Apparently, there has always been a remnant. Many were, and still are blinded by a spirit of stupor, causing eyes not to see, and ears not to hear their God. For sure, many are still blind and deaf spiritually right now.

There is more going on in God's eyes concerning what He has planned to do with the time of the Gentiles. They will come into the Kingdom before the Jewish people. This chapter reveals the plan of God, that He has an order, or an appointed time in His Kingdom that we may not understand. His plan does not reject His Chosen People, no matter how they have historically rejected Him. We will listen to His Word and try to understand and believe for the salvation of the Jews.

Paul cries out, "*... they did not stumble so as to fall, did they? May it never be! But in their transgression salvation has come to the Gentiles, to make them jealous.*"

"*... a partial hardening has happened to all Israel until the fulness of the Gentiles has come in; and thus allIsrael will be saved, just as it is written, <u>'THE DELIVERER WILL COME FROM ZION. HE WILL REMOVE UNGODLINESS FROM JACOB, AND THIS IS MY COVENANT WITH THEM, WHEN I TAKE AWAY THEIR SINS.'</u>*"

We, at such a time as this, have so much to learn as we continue to mine deeply in the Word of God, such as in the book of Revelation. From the prophetic revelation, it appears that many others and I are hearing that the end times are rapidly approaching. We are about to see what we have never imagined in the very near future.

What about today? How do we live to the fullest, manifesting our destiny every moment we are still on this earth? I will look and listen for more intimate and timely revelation every day that I am still alive; how about you? Even today, I cry out to you to know the Lord more intimately every day, whether those days be many or few. Lord, we ask You to make us ready to meet You and each other in the air —or in Heaven.

Shalom for now!

4

———————

WHO IS MY ENEMY?

The Bible answers our question by first telling us who our enemies are not! They are not who we thought they were – flesh and blood human beings!

And then it tells us who our enemies are – a hierarchy of supernatural entities most of us have never heard of, even if we have been in church all our lives!

Certainly, no government or news media understands this, although many of them are controlled by these beings! Only our God truly understands, so we are going to have to get our news and strategy from Him and His Bible if we ever hope to win this supernatural war we are all in. Wow!

Here we go mining for truth again, but this time we are going way beyond just this world! Get ready to go from the center of the earth to the highest heavens, supernaturally!

Let's start with the most important revelatory biblical passage on the subject and see if we can learn who these evil supernatural entities are and how to win over them. Buckle up for quite a ride! We'll start by looking at the meaning of the words in the original Greek language of the New Testament and see if a more complete translation helps us understand who these enemies are.

Mark key words as you read, like "wrestle," "kingdom of darkness," "fallen angels," "chiefs of angels," "this age," and "Kosmosrator" so you can study and understand the battle. I was never taught about this battle in church and I doubt that you were either. Our leaders were as clueless as we are! No wonder we are all struggling to understand why horrible things in our nation and in the world are happening! If we don't learn who our enemies are, how can we expect to win the battle for ourselves, our families or our nations?

Ephesians 6:12 NKJV

... we do not wrestle against flesh and blood, but against

1. *Principalities*[1] - #746 in Strong's Concordance: *Arche* in Greek - ruling authorities; princes or chiefs of angels: the beginning and extremity of

---

1. I used the following resources for a more complete definition of the Greek words in this passage: The New Strong's Exhaustive Concordance of the Bible, The Complete Word Study Dictionary, New Testament, by Spiros Zodhiates, Th.D., The Complete Word Study New Testament, by Spiros Zodhiates, Th.D., including Lexical Aids to the New Testament.

rule, authority, power and dominion of the kingdom of darkness.

2. *Powers* - #1849 in Strong's Concordance: *Exousia* in Greek – superhuman potentates, fallen angels who have right and might, power, dominion, ability and authority to do evil over persons and things.

3. *The rulers of the darkness of this age* –*#2888 in* Strong's Concordance: *Kosmokrator* - plural in Greek in this passage – Satan and his fallen angels. **Note that they are tolerated by God for only this age**, giving everyone a chance to get delivered from their illegitimate rule in the darkness and turn to the Light of Jesus.

4. *Spiritual forces of wickedness in the heavenly places.* - #2032 in Strong's Concordance: *Epouranios* in Greek – "above the sky." These fallen angels are headquartered in what we call the Second Heaven and other dimensions, including under the earth, where they have been kicked out of Heaven because of their iniquity.

But don't forget that if you are born again into the Kingdom of God, your spirit man is already seated far above all evil spirits, in Christ Jesus, as an important part of His body. All evil fallen angels of every rank are under your feet![2]

Let's very briefly review the biblical history of mankind's

---

2. Ephesians 1:18-23, Romans 16:20

fall and why these evil enemies have any power at all over any human:

YHWH Elohim, the one and only true God of all creation, gave dominion over the whole earth to Adam and Eve, the first humans He created. They were to rule under His ultimate authority with only one rule to obey, as we have already discussed. **Satan became the god of this world for a set time determined by the true God because Adam and Eve sinned and gave their dominion to him.**[3]

Never forget that Jesus totally defeated Satan and all his cohorts on the cross. But the true God never revoked free will or the penalty for sin. Everyone on earth must make a choice of whom he worships, either the Kingdom of God: God the Father, Jesus (Yeshua) and Holy Spirit or Satan and his kingdom.

So, through deception and witchcraft, *Kosmokrators*, Satan and his kingdom, still fight the true God and His Kingdom for control of this world system for as long as He allows them to! Tragically, the majority of the descendants of Adam and Eve have chosen to continue to follow and worship Satan and his fallen angels. We are also still battling the entire wicked hierarchy of Principalities, Powers, Kosmokrators and Spiritual forces of wickedness in heavenly places. But God!

As revealed throughout the Bible, Satan's kingdom is led by an evil trinity made up of Satan,[4] Queen of Heaven

---

3. Genesis 1:27-28; 2:15-17; 3:6,22-24; 2 Corinthians 4:4
4. I John 5:19

(Mystery Babylon)[5] **and Antichrist.**[6] (Much more about this in later chapters) They lurk in malicious wickedness, commonly called the Kingdom of Darkness.

As complicated as this looks, understand that there are only these two kingdoms. But the Kingdom of Darkness is mysterious on purpose through the deception of hierarchies of at least hundreds of gods and goddesses disguised by multiple names, religions, and languages! Be sure that you understand that mythology is **all fiction,** so don't allow yourself to be further confused by it. Real satanic structures are a whole different thing.

Times are coming when Satan, the Antichrist Beast, the False Prophet, Death, Hades, and anyone whose name is not written in the Lamb's Book of Life will find his destiny in eternal condemnation and punishment "in the Lake of Fire and Brimstone."[7] Man's issue about who he worships is definitely no game. Each one's choice will determine where and how he spends eternity - in the glorious bliss of eternity with his loving God or in the Lake of Fire with all the wicked fallen angels in eternal torment.

This passage makes the distinction "of this age"! The Kingdom of Darkness' time on earth is limited and their eternal judgment is at a fixed time and forever.

Even though Jesus totally defeated Satan on the cross,[8]

---

5. Revelation 17:18
6. Revelation 13:7-8
7. Revelation 20:10-15
8. Matthew 28:18

the evil one still rules the wicked, demonic world structure during this era. The mercy and longsuffering patience of our true God is still calling every person alive to repent and turn to Him as his God. He is not willing that any should perish,[9] but sadly, most will! This age, when our God is calling us all to repentance and forgiveness for sin, will not last forever. Time is rapidly running out!

The Bible says it this way in 2 Corinthians 4:4: "Satan, the god of this world," because most of the people in the world right now are deceived by and follow the will of Satan for their lives, in rebellion to the true God.

In the Greek, the word for "world" is #165 is *aidn*. This word actually means age or time. During this age, humans are given the choice whether or not to worship the true God, but the false gods of deceived humans are in no way truly other Gods. They are, at most, only fallen creations[10] of the one true God. But, because of free will, humans can choose to allow Satan and his Kingdom of Darkness to deceive them and be their gods they trust and worship. But if they make this choice, their gods will lead them to the lake of fire with them.[11] Only the one and only true God makes this call.

Our God who is Perfect Love never intended this to happen, He created us to live forever in a paradise and would have expanded the garden to the whole world. But sin

---

9.   2 Peter 3:9

10.   Revelation 12:7-9

11.   Revelation 20:11-15

changed everything.[12] In spite of the Fall and throughout this whole age, He gives everyone time to turn to Him to forgive their sins and save them for eternal life with Him. Jesus became a man, died on the cross and resurrected from the grave to make our salvation possible.[13] The question is whether we will bow the knee to Him as God and go to heaven with Him or bow to fallen angels as gods and spend eternity in the lake of fire with them! Everyone makes his own personal choice.

As we have discussed before, our God does not want robots for His children or for His Son's Bride, so he gives man free will to choose to believe Him or lies. We can obey Him and receive eternal life and joy or rebel against Him and pay the price of the eternal lake of fire.

During this age and during our lifetime, we can decide where we will spend eternity. All rebels follow a hierarchy of fallen angels, even if they have no idea who they are!

After this age, everything changes! There is no such thing in existence as a man who is in charge. That mindset is a total lie. Read the Book of Revelation to see the magnitude of the point I am making. Everyone bows to God or the gods of the Kingdom of Darkness, destined for the lake of fire with all who worship them. We all choose our God or gods who are going to burn forever in total torment with all their followers!

There is a new heaven and new earth coming and pure joy

---

12. Genesis 3
13. Isaiah 53:5; I Peter 2:24

and blessings for all who give their lives to the one and only true God. But there is eternal judgment for all who rejected the salvation offered by the cross of Jesus. All who refuse to accept Jesus as their Savior for sin will pay the eternal price for rejecting Him.

If you are a born-again believer, you are seated at the right hand of Father God, even now, ruling and reigning with Jesus, where no evil spirit has any authority or access. They are all under your feet, including Satan and every one of these powerful fallen angels we just identified, plus all their underlings. They are not only under our feet, but also on their way to eternal damnation because of the finished work of our precious LORD and Savior Jesus' blood sacrifice for our sin. Hallelujah! No fear of any fallen angel or lesser demon. They are all defeated by the cross.

What a relief! Those fallen angels seem scary and overwhelming until we stop and realize who our God is and what he has already totally overcome once and for all for us. We win big time! This is because the battle has already been won on the cross. Jesus arose from the dead and ascended to the right hand of Father where we now sit with and in Him. And we now rule and reign with Him. He is the Head and we are part of His body, all seated with Father God.[14]

One day all our enemies will be judged permanently. Hallelujah!

If you are feeling convicted and afraid as you are reading

---

14. Ephesians 1:18-2:6

this, I have good news for you: You can repent of your sins, be saved and join the Family of God. He died for you, too.

Maybe you are saved, but are being convicted that something between you and your Lord is not resolved. If so, I recommend that you ask your Lord to lead you to a Spirit-filled deliverance ministry who is trained and gifted to seek the Lord with you to take care of your need to make things, possibly personally and generationally, right with Him.

If you are from certain parts of the world, like Africa, you are very familiar with evil spirits and have no trouble with these concepts about evil spirits because your world view is supernatural. But you still need to find the right person to help you. Not everything supernatural is God, and we can all be deceived by demonic entities pretending to be from the true God. Wherever you are from, be sure to stay in the Word and test every spirit to be sure it is from God.

In the western world, where we think we are so smart and in charge, we are generally woefully ignorant of different hierarchies of spirits who truly war against us and the true God. They control most people's minds and world view, world-wide right now in this age! If you doubt me, just look at our government, listen to main stream news or look at the curriculums of our schools. Or just ask a politician, "What is a woman?" They don't even know anymore! That is how much their minds have been taken over by evil spirits! They are not just ignorant. They are possessed or at least oppressed by spirits they have given themselves to by their lifestyle, beliefs and worship! And many of these deceived people are running the nations today!

These categories of supernatural spirit beings we have been looking at who have brainwashed many people's minds are actually the high level fallen angels and their hierarchies. They are not unlike the watcher angels who rebelled against God and fell from heaven deliberately because of their lust for human women. They invaded Earth to mate with beautiful women and sire children! They might even be a part of this hierarchy today. I don't know for sure how the angels are organized now.

But we do know that these watcher angels who fell's offspring were the giants (Nephalim in Hebrew) recorded in Genesis 6, all through the Bible[15] and in much more detail in the apocryphal Book of I Enoch.[16] And we know that we need to understand them because we must study the categories of enemy angels we just looked at from Ephesians. See the biblical references listed in the footnote below.

These fallen angels so perverted culture and the human gene pool that God had to destroy the earth by the flood![17] He was only able to save Noah and his family so that the gene pool would not be so polluted with Nephalim genes (half human/half fallen angel) that Jesus could never be born as a true human to save mankind!

Is our world approaching this level of evil again? Does this

---

15. Genesis 6; Numbers 13:30-33; Deuteronomy 2:19,11,20; 3:11-12; Joshua 12:4, 13:12, 13:8, 17:15, 18:16; 2 Samuel 21:16; 18, 20,22; I Chronicles 28:4,6; 20:8; Job 16:14; I Peter3:19; 2 Peter3:4; Jude 1:6; 5; 6
16. First Enoch, Translated by R.H. Charles D. LITT. D.D. Chapters 6-16, 19, 66:4-23, 69.
17. Genesis 6:4-22

sound important enough for us to make sure that we understand these biblical passages and the huge evil supernatural hierarchy the Bible teaches in Ephesians, in Genesis 6 and throughout the Bible? Religion has so dumbed down most churches through infiltration by deceiving spirits that few have a clue of what we are talking about. I doubt that 5% of the people who claim to be believers have even read the Bible! How tragic, especially now when we are again approaching what the Bible calls the days of Noah![18]

All throughout the Old Testament, we read the history of Israel's refusal to totally deal with these fallen angel offspring they found inhabiting their Promised Land.

They not only didn't obey God and totally eliminate them from their land, as God had commanded them to do. They married into these defiled bloodlines, worshiped their fallen angel gods and birthed their children, thereby mixing the Abrahamic bloodlines with the horrid Nephalim bloodlines. (The word Nephalim is Hebrew for giants.[19])

This major issue is the primary reason that Israel as a nation has never accepted and even crucified her Messiah! If you read the Book of Revelation, you will see that Israel ultimately thinks that the wicked Antichrist is her Messiah and follows him till mid-tribulation, when he goes into the temple and declares himself God. As we have already seen,

---

18. Matthew 24:37-44
19. Genesis 6:1-4;9

both Egypt and Assyria come into the Kingdom of God before Israel! What a price she pays because she refused to obey God and wipe out all the Nephalim evil ones who led her astray

For a shocking example of the personal consequence of mixed Nephalim bloodlines, let's look at King David: (I'll bet you have never heard this part of David's life! I hadn't either until I started digging more deeply! It makes a lot of David's family's tragic lives make more sense.)

David married Maaca[20] and Absalom was their son. But you probably don't know who her father was. **The father of Maaca was a giant Nephalim** descendant! This defiled, mixed bloodline through Maaca and David might have had a lot to do with Absalom's disposition toward sexual abominations and rebellion against his father[21] that ended in his tragic death[22] while trying to overthrow David's Kingdom. Perhaps the sexual relationship between David

---

20. According to the Shalve/Hyman Encyclopedia of Jewish Women, Maacah was captured by David in war, strictly because of lust for her. And he made her his wife. Absalom was their son. Maacah was a non-Jewish woman and the Rabbis blamed David's behavior for Absalom's issues. Even though David was a man God said was after His own heart, he fell into multiple sexual sins. Tragically for the whole family, the results were disastrous. His adultery with Bathsheba led to his plan that murdered her husband and probably caused the death of their child. For all of us studying these issues, we need to see how David wrestled and the price he and his family suffered as a result of his generational sexual issues. Even though he was truly repentant, we must see the effects of his generational iniquities and seek deliverance from our own generational personal issues.

21. 2 Samuel 15:1-20

22. 2 Samuel 18:9-33

and his wife with Nephalim blood and generational iniquities was also a factor and open door to David and his children's horrible sexual issues of incest[23] and adultery!

These issues in David's day have been continually ongoing through the ages through generational iniquitous mindsets, especially propagated in the Illuminati and Nephalim fallen angel bloodlines. These generational, horrific behaviors even walk out more openly today as satanic ritual abuse, the sacrifice of innocent babies we call abortion and the hideous, huge practice of pedophilia and sex-traffick-

---

23. 2 Samuel 13: Note that Tamar who was raped was the daughter of Maacha and David, the sister of Absalom and the granddaughter of Maacha's father who was a Nephalim giant descendant of the fallen angels. David was never willing to deal with the rape and shameful exposure of his daughter Tamar by his son, Amnon, even though Maacha and Absalom confronted him for justice! Tamar's whole life was ruined and she lived in shame that was not her fault at all, and David did nothing! Her brother Absalom was horrified at his father's seeming indifference. So, after David refused to initiate any form of justice, Absalom took justice in his own hands and killed his half-brother, the rapist. David would never reconcile with Absalom after that so he fled back to his mother's people. I assume that he went to live with his Nephalim grandfather, but I don't know for sure. It was 3 years before David even allowed him to return. I do not know if his grandfather was still alive, but it is very doubtful that these people were at all a godly influence. Even after all this time, David would not reconcile to him or let him live with him. Absalom's heart was further crushed. After David was confronted about his behavior against Absalom, there was a brief attempted reconciliation, but it was apparently too little, too late, and the resulting rebellion of Absalom was tragically fatal for him and heart breaking for David. None of these family tragedies and iniquities were ever resolved in David's life, even though he loved God, sought after Him and privately grieved over his sons. What a lesson to teach us the necessity of personal deliverance from generational iniquities if we want our families healed and protected!

ing. I remind you again of the US today. And the church is largely clueless!

If we ever hope to overcome the abominations happening today, we must understand the roots of these generational iniquities, including the supernatural fallen angel connection. And we must repent and be delivered from their legal iniquitous influence we and our forefathers have given them.

This supernatural battle with fallen angels is the battle we in the U.S. are in right now! We are witnessing evil in the highest levels in government, education, family, law, art, media, business, entertainment and even religion. Those of us who are older never would have believed we would experience anything like this, at least not out in the open involving the highest levels of society. We truly do not wrestle with flesh and blood, but we are controlled by fallen angels in high places that we do not see as the root cause of all the wicked transformation of all the facets of society I just mentioned! And we struggle under our generational curses from Nephalim forefathers 99.9 % of even Christians have no understanding of!

People do study mythology and are influenced by the fantasy supernatural, the better to confuse you, my dear! But real fallen angels and demons are very dangerous, deadly, always lie and never die! You will find them wickedly manifesting everywhere, especially politically! Just turn on your TV and ask God to open your spiritual eyes to see what is truly manifesting there, seeking to deceive you with every word spoken!

We can never win this wrestling match in ignorance or without learning to work with our true God's greater supernatural power through Holy Spirit and His angel armies.

Only Holy spirit, who has been kicked out of many churches, can empower us to win over the lesser hierarchy of fallen angels who are on their way to eternal damnation and punishment.

We must learn to fight in heavenly places in Christ Jesus far above all fallen angels. Jesus is the victorious God-man who has totally defeated every fallen angel and has all authority and power to defeat every supernatural foe.

He is our Head and has chosen and paid in full for us to be His body. We are seated with Him in the high and holy place of immeasurable power and authority at the right hand of Father God.

Holy Spirit has gifted us with Heaven's power. And He is fully equipping us to totally defeat all the power of every fallen angel of any rank. In Jesus, we can't lose. We are far above all these fallen angels and they are all destined for eternal damnation. Just read the Book of Revelation.

Reality is that a constant battle for the eternal life of every human is going on between the Kingdom of God versus the Kingdom of Satan (Darkness) all day every day in the unseen world all around us! LORD, please open our spiritual eyes to see reality.

Now, let's stop for a minute and access where each of us individually is in our understanding. How are you doing on our supernatural mining expedition? It's certainly not boring, is it? Are you seeing anything new as we look into dimensions you may not have ever studied before? Once you see these other dimensions, the evil all around the world suddenly starts making perfect sense!

But if you've never seen anything like this before, it can be scary and unnerving. Don't be afraid. But do be open to dramatic change, if that is where our LORD is leading you.

The most important reality is that where we spend eternity will be determined by the outcome of this personal spiritual battle between us and the supernatural beings we encounter in each one of our human lives. I hope that you all are seeing that there is actually no contest between our God and the fallen angel gods. They are all under our feet and destined for the lake of fire. But we must learn to war. Passivity and ignorance will never win any battle. And the battle is escalating exponentially.

Only understanding this critical reality will equip us to learn the seriousness of the battle we are in and why we need the armor of God explained in Ephesians 6:10-18.

Because you are in a spiritual battle 24/7/365 days a year and the battle is intensifying every day in the highest places of authority on earth, you need to put on spiritual armor every day if you do not want to be wounded, possibly even fatally!

This passage in Ephesians 6, using the imagery of a wrestling match, was written in Greek to an audience who were accustomed to Greek wrestling matches – totally different from our wrestling shows. Theirs were real battles, often to the death! In the end, the victor stood over his opponent with his foot on the neck of his defeated foe, possibly even dead, lying on the ground, proving who was the victor. It was no show!

And our wrestling with Satan is also no show! We are just generally clueless about what is happening to us when we think we are getting by with rebellion against the laws of God!

So, this passage instructs us to deliberately put on the spiritual armor of God if we want to win our battles with Satan and his vast and supernaturally evil army.

Since Satan is like a roaring lion, seeking whom he may devour, let's look at each piece. We must understand how to protect ourselves and win. We also want to learn how to protect our loved ones and fight for our nation and world that is in serious peril right now, primarily due to total ignorance of the vast majority of people about our enemies and the spiritual battle every single human must fight. Tragically, most of the church is included in the spiritually blind! Be sure that you understand that our ignorance is no accident, but the result of deliberate invasions of churches by evil people and spirits hell bent on keeping us from understanding the supernatural, spiritual warfare and our spiritual position in the heavenlies as Jesus' body. They have even convinced much of the church that the supernatural gifts of Holy Spirit that were the very essence of the early church's supernatural power and miraculous success no longer exist. This is a horrible heresy.

We must understand that if we do not fight with wisdom and spiritual armor and weapons, we lose by default! Nobody is exempt from the war, and those who are in the most danger are those who do not believe what I'm telling you. Let's learn God's strategy for war and His divine protection pictured as armor and also learn how to access His main supernatural weapon:

Armor of God: Ephesians 6:13-20

1. **Belt of Truth** - All the other pieces of armor attach to this one. It is critical to victory. We must know our Bible if we don't want to lose to Satan – especially today when if our enemies are moving their mouths, they are lying! **The major media networks are brainwashing every listener with nothing but heinous lies and every technique of deception and mind control imaginable! I loved it when Tucker Carlson played the talking points of the numerous main stream liberal networks. They all repeated the same words every time, obviously reading from the script their lying bosses gave them all to repeat like robots! To the horror of every sane person, even our children in public schools financed by our taxes, are being taught such heresy that the children are told that they can decide which sex they are supposed to be!** Then they, by the masses, are undergoing irreversible surgery and hormone therapy **to**

destroy their God-given sexual and emotional identity! And we wonder why many commit suicide! I have a close friend whose beautiful granddaughter at age 9 "became a boy!" People, no human by himself comes up with this evil. It takes fallen angel supernaturally possessed people to think this stuff up! Worse yet, they are able to legally brainwash little children with this hell without telling the parents because our government and schools are also now under the control of the evil ones!! Wicked lies have gotten so prolific that now little children are trained in public schools paid for by our taxes, to believe that every white person is born racist and deserves to be punished and treated as despicable and responsible for every societal evil, from birth. The white children are even being left out of field trips and brainwashed in self-hatred as wicked racists! These evil, lying politicians are the racists! They need to look in the mirror! Truth is under siege like never before, so be sure to always wear this crucial piece of armor.

2. **Breastplate of Righteousness** – This piece of armor protects your heart and vital organs. Today in such a diabolically evil governmental structure, our hearts are constantly under siege. **The hearts and minds of thousands of powerful leaders are totally demonically possessed! But everyone, no matter how deceived and demonized they are, can be delivered and set free.**

3. **Shoes that prepare you to walk in shalom peace** wherever you go to spread the gospel of the Kingdom of God. **Without supernatural armor, shalom is impossible.** With our God in total control, nothing is missing or broken in our spirits and souls and our bodies will respond to His healing power. Walk in confidence that our God has us protected as we walk with and for Him.

4. **Shield of Faith** - Be sure to cover your whole body with the huge shield of faith, saturated with the water of the Word, so that **truth extinguishes the fiery darts of the enemy continually plummeting your faith with poison darts and arrows of pure deception.**

5. **Helmet of Salvation** - Your mind must be protected by the impenetrable helmet of salvation so that you always agree with the mind of Christ Jesus and never with the heresy of the liar.

6. **Sword of the Spirit** - Now you are truly ready for your offensive weapon – the sword of the Spirit, which is the Word of God. With it you can block every stab aimed at your heart or back or the heart of even the weakest victim the enemy is trying to take out. But **you only have this weapon if you know the Word of God! If you are ignorant of the Word, you have no offensive weapon!** But I have good news for you if you are horrified at this reality in your life: You can repent today and get ready to win the war! Remember who you are. If you know the LORD, you are seated in heavenly places in Christ Jesus. He's the Head and you are

part of His body. Be ready to do your part in His battle for the Kingdom of God, yourself, your family and the world. **Be armed and dangerous to every enemy that tries to take you and the nations out! Sharpen your sword by studying the Word every day.**

Don't ever forget how you have been or can be transformed and seated in the heavenly places as a part of Jesus' body. Once you are saved, He calls you to be baptized in water to picture your death, burial and resurrection and also be baptized in Holy Spirit to transform you into the supernaturally powerful new creation Jesus died to make you.

Holy Spirit baptism by Jesus empowers you to be not just born again, but transformed into the new creation Yeshua died to change you into for the glory of the Father.

Jesus told His disciples that He must go so Holy Spirit could come and finish the transformation the whole Trinity of Father, Son and Holy Spirit must complete. He came to earth to change us into New Creations never before seen, empowered by Holy Spirit for the glory of Father God. Remember that you were created to be supernatural!

Totally transformed by Father, Son and Holy Spirit, you definitely will not lose. No matter how bad it gets, we always win as Jesus' body – new creations, armored up as Holy Spirit's supernatural army in total obedience to Father! We are more than conquerors. We are literally Super Man in Christ Jesus! He is the Head and we are the body!

The Big Picture

According to the Bible, there are only two kingdoms! The evil ones have numerous names and players, but that is mostly the better to confuse you and make you think the hierarchy of evil is much more complicated and powerful than it is.

Actually, there is only the Kingdom of God (Kingdom of Light) and the Kingdom of Satan (Kingdom of Darkness). For simplicity's sake, that is the good news. But there is also bad news we must understand in order to win the battle with the evil ones:

There Is an Innumerable Number of Angels[24]
One Third of the Angels Fell from Heaven
and Joined Satan's Kingdom

This fact is bad news, because 1/3 of an innumerable number is still an innumerable number. But the best news is that their leaders, including Satan, are just fallen angels kicked out of Heaven.

If we are saved, our Leader is the Creator and God of all created things and beings. We are in Jesus as part of His body and seated in Him far above all fallen angels, including Satan. No worries, no contest, no fear! They are all

---

24. Hebrews 12:22

headed for eternal hell and punishment. We, our God and all the angels who have not betrayed our God are now warring for us and we will spend eternity together in joy, peace and love. I believe that this era on earth will soon be over! And what happens after this world is no more is absolutely unbelievably awesome or more catastrophic than anyone could imagine. Stay tuned till the end of the story.

Hierarchy of Two Kingdoms

**Satan Is Never Original, but an Expert Counterfeiter
You Can Look at the Structure of Any False Religion and
See His Variations on the Theme,
Repeated Over and Over.**

**Let's Look at the True Trinity versus
Satan's End Time Counterfeit Trinity**

Kingdom of God		Kingdom of Satan	
	Father		Satan
Son	Holy Spirit	Antichrist	Queen of Heaven

The Bible clearly tells us that man has been given free will since the very beginning of creation. Remember that we said that God did this because He does not want robots, but faithful sons and daughters who truly love Him.

We have also learned that Jesus died for us so we can be forgiven for our sins and redeemed from the curse, even when we don't deserve it. (We never do.) And the Bible says that God is longsuffering, patient and kind and gives us time to repent. These biblical principles and the character of God explain why God doesn't just put us and Satan and all his fallen angels in hell the first time we cross Him.

He gives us free will to choose to love and worship Him or follow the evil ones. And, during this age we live in, He gives us time to be sure of the path we will ultimately choose. One day, probably much sooner than we expect, "this age" is over and His just judgement of every person and angel manifests. Finally, we see Him create a New Heaven and New Earth and just judgement of every angel and person who ever lived fully manifests. Are you and I ready?

Now, let's look at our other choice - the structure of Satan and his counterfeit gods' world system. Following them is an option for every man and angel, and tragically, most humans and 1/3 of the angels make this tragic choice!

These counterfeit gods rule the whole worldly structure during the age when the one and only true Creator God allows them to manifest their lies so that man has a free will choice to decide who he wants to spend eternity with! Remember, the true Creator God is Perfect Love and love that is not voluntary is not love. Tragically, most people will choose Satan and his fallen angels to worship. Listen to what the Word says about their Kingdom of Darkness!

Satan

I John 5:19 NASB
"... the whole world lies in the power of the evil one"

II Corinthians 4:4 NASB
"the god of this world has blinded the minds of the unbelieving."

Queen of Heaven

Revelation 17:18 Amplified Study Bible

"The woman whom you saw is the great city, which reigns over and dominates and controls the kings and the political leaders of the earth."

This whole biblical concept of the Queen of Heaven, Mystery Babylon, is truly a difficult mystery to understand. Let's try by untangling it as much as possible. This woman is the great city, as this reference tells you, but biblically, she is also so much more.

She is also the Queen of Heaven, Great Harlot, Babylon the Great, the Mother of Harlots (Revelation 17:1,5) She is called a city, but don't let that trip you up! The Bride of Christ is also called a city, the New Jerusalem! (Revelation 21:9,10)

So, **this mysterious woman has a spiritual place, a demonic system, a physically inhabited place or places and is an evil spirit!** I interpret these mysterious clues to indicate that we are looking at **a very evil spirit operating and hiding behind a demonic system and in a primary city.** In Revelation 18, the most critical scripture on this subject, we get a whole lot more revelation about this mystery.

Read Revelation 18 and take notes.

The Bible talks about kings having sex with this spirit. You can't have sex with a city, so the plot thickens as we try to unravel the mystery of this biblical language.

To me, it makes more sense to focus on the spirit and spiritual meanings behind the demonic system and city than to try and understand the complicated and confusing word pictures.

The literal meaning of the word translated "reigns" in Revelation 17:18 is "has a kingdom." So, we might write **our own amplified version of this verse** to say, **"The high-level supernatural woman, the Spirit of Harlotry, the Queen of Heaven, Babylon the Great, the Mother of Harlots, is a spirit who has a kingdom over the kings of the earth."**

In Revelation 17:1,15, this reality is poetically depicted as she sits on many waters, representing people, multitudes, nations and tongues.

My current summary would say that there is a very high-level spiritual being, the Spirit of Harlotry, influencing

almost every king and many leaders on earth with her demonic power and agenda, particularly using sexual immorality of every imaginable kind to capture them in her claws. Why else would she be called the Spirit of Harlotry?

She has a supernatural authority that supersedes that of the kings of the earth to the degree that they serve her, wittingly or unwittingly.

This Harlot gains her authority through empowering illicit, supernatural sexual behavior "with her"! Victims usually have no idea at all that sexual immorality is a deadly supernatural trap they are falling into and will possibly never survive, eternally! The vast majority of the church has o understanding of how to set these captives free, even though in Christ Jesus, total deliverance is absolutely available to anyone who is willing to truly repent and stop living in harlotry!

Today, this sexual, hellish bondage commonly starts with innocent little children who are targeted by wicked, demonized adults who have usually been similarly abused themselves. It may be as hidden and personal as a father or mother abusing only his or her own child or as organized in the highest-level satanic ritual abuse ring in the world.

Consequentially, the level of damage to the child will range from hellish generational abuse to the highest level of satanic programming, starting as an innocent child and continuing and deepening for a whole lifetime! The victim may even be deliberately, massively dissociated and programmed to do all sorts of heinous crimes for the cult through multiple programmed, dissociated parts who have no idea what they are doing!

I could write a whole book on this subject, but let me just list a few more ways this spirit destroys millions of individuals who are trapped in sexual bondage. There are vast multitudes of open doors to this hell! It can happen through pornography and evil media, pedophilia, sexual abuse, Satanic ritual abuse, actual voluntary sexual harlotry, masturbation, fantasy and mind control, to mention a few traps.

What almost nobody understands is that any of the above plus a whole lot more legally open a person to a lifetime of hellish control over that person's sexuality by the spirit of harlotry. Without major deliverance and inner healing, it will be impossible for that person to have a godly, normal marriage or life! But God! But deliverance!

It can even get worse if the victim connects with a witch or warlock who understands operating through mind control and astral projection and is trained to demonically overpower and further destroy godly sex in this victim's marriage!

The mind control is to turn the person against his or her spouse and toward the witch or warlock empowered by Satan to kill, steal and destroy the victim of sexual wickedness empowered by this spirit.

The spirit of harlotry is so diabolically evil that <u>she is responsible for all the slain in the earth and she is so well hidden that in the the Bible, she says that nobody sees her!</u>[25]

<u>All of this wickedness requires the enemies the Bible revealed to us in Ephesians 6. None of this could be manifested through humans alone!</u>

I hope that my explanation helps make this difficult passage a little clearer.

The Antichrist
(Also Biblically Known as the Beast)
The Third Member of the Kingdom of Darkness

Revelation 13:1-8

The **dragon (Satan)** gave him **(the beast, the Antichrist)** his power and his throne and great authority.

And they worshiped the **dragon, (Satan)** because he gave his authority to the **beast (the Antichrist).**

It was given to him **(the Antichrist)** to make war with **the saints** and to overcome them, and authority over **every tribe and nation** was given to him, **everyone whose name has not been written from the foundation of the world in the book of life of the Lamb** who has been slain **(Jesus).**

---

25. Isaiah 47:1-11

Everyone on earth at that end time who is not a true Christian will worship the Antichrist!

All three: Satan, Babylon the Great, the great Mother of Harlots, the Spirit of Harlotry and the Antichrist have universal authority and are interrelated.

For example, Satan gives the Antichrist his power (Revelation 13:1) and the Great Harlot sits on the Beast (Antichrist) Revelation 17: 3)

I believe that these three form the core leadership of the Babylonian Kingdom in direct opposition to Jesus and the Kingdom of God. They form the counterfeit false trinity and Kingdom of Darkness. Remember, there are only two kingdoms!

The better to deliberately confuse you, My Dear! I believe we see variations on this theme of counterfeit gods and goddesses in a great multitude of false religions and myths that mock the true trinity and lead millions astray, worshiping fallen angels who are plotting to be worshiped.

Again, mythology mimics all sorts of variations of these real battles with the fallen angels. These supernatural myths are really meant to deceive you about the real battle with real enemies. Flee from all mythology, all of which will just lead you to demonic counterfeits of the real supernatural enemies!

When I look around the world at the magnitude of deceptions of the fallen angels receiving worship, especially today, I am horrified! Look at the statistics:

World Religions[26]

Christianity 31.1%
Islam 24.9%
Irreligion 15.6%
Hinduism 15.2%
Buddhism 6.6%
Folk Religion 5,6%
Other 1%

I find this chart terrifying! The eternally critical question is, "How many of these people are truly worshiping the one and only true God who will take them to Heaven with Him forever and how many are worshiping His arch enemies who will suffer with them in the eternal lake of fire?"

Please make sure that you are not one of their deceived victims!

____

26. en.m.wikipedia.org

5

WHAT IS MY ENEMY'S STRATEGY?

According to the Bible, on the planet earth during this era, we have three main wicked enemies trying to challenge the one and only true God and win every human over to worship them as the gods who rule this universe. Their goal is to kill, steal and destroy God's creation in every way possible.[1]

OK, miners, we are going to have to go further underground and deeper into darkness than ever before to un-

---

1. Three enemies who rule the whole earth for this era:
   Satan: I John 5:19 NASB *"The whole world lies in the power of the evil one."*
   The Great Harlot: Revelation 7:1 NASB *"... Come here, I will show you the judgment of the great harlot ...." "The woman whom you saw ... reigns (has a kingdom) over the kings of the earth."*
   Antichrist, Beast: Revelation 13:7-8 NASB *"... Authority over every tribe and people and tongue and nation was given to him. All who dwell on the earth will worship him, everyone whose name has not been written in the Book of Life of the Lamb who has been slain."*

cover their strategy. This territory can get complicated, spooky, and just plain weird! Are you ready? Let's go!

SATAN

- **One Enemy Everybody Has Heard Of**
- **His Numerous Biblical Names Help Unmask His Strategy.**
- **He Is also Called the Following Names:**
  - **The Devil**
  - **The Serpent of Old**
  - **The Great Dragon**
  - **The Ruler of this Age, and**
  - **The Leader of the Kingdom of Darkness –Kosmokrator (Greek)**

We were introduced to this chief enemy on earth during this age in Chapter 4, as we were confronted by Ephesians 6:12. That passage shocked us into realizing that our enemies are not the wicked people we thought they were, but a fallen angel hierarchy that we were basically clueless about. Remember, we learned that Satan is called a "Kosmokrator" in the Greek and he leads the third group of fallen angels listed in that passage. He rules over the false trinity, called "the Kingdom of Darkness of this Age," and all their demonic underlings.

Who Was Satan before and after His Fall?
How Did He Fall?
What Is His Plan for You and Me Now?[2]

Ezekiel 28:1-19 Amplified Study Bible
This Ezekiel Passage is the
Human King's Battle with Satan
The Fall of the Human Prince of Tyre

---

2.   I am going to quote most of this key passage about the fall of Satan and how he can control and possess mankind, even resulting in the destruction of political rulers and their kingdoms without anyone having a clue about what is really going on.

This biblical account is an additional revelation like Ephesians 6, giving us an historic example of how we do not wrestle with humans, but with a hierarchy of high level supernatural fallen angels.

The scariest part of this Old Testament passage is that, generally speaking, the church today still does not know any more than this ancient ruler knew about the supernatural! His mind had been totally taken over by Satan and he had no idea that he was believing preposterous lies that ultimately would destroy him! In fact, governmental leaders today may be even more deceived than he was! But these huge deceptions only work if people are believing Satan, the liar. Yikes! My line of reasoning is getting too close to today's governmental situations world-wide for comfort!

Please take this training in the Bible very seriously for your own life, understanding that not only political rulers and their kingdoms are targeted by principalities and powers, but also you and me, our families and friends and our lands.

Never forget that the outcome for everyone and every place will depend on their relationship and obedience to God.

One God is in control of ALL and only His rules determine the eternal destiny of us all. There is just one God and He is LOVE, but agape love of God is not sloppy and tolerant of evil. Evil behavior results in eternal consequences for all of God's creation, including you and me and our families. So, let's mine the Scriptures and see what we can learn about the eternal consequences of our understanding of our enemies.

"... Son of man, say to the **<u>prince of Tyre</u>,**[3] *'Thus says the Lord God, "... your heart is lifted up and* **you have said and thought, 'I am a god. I sit in the seat of the gods ...'** *yet you are [only] a man ... and not God.*

Though you ... think your mind is [as wise as] the mind of God — behold, you are [imagining yourself] wiser than Daniel; there is no secret [you think] hidden from you. With your [own] wisdom and with your [own] understanding you have acquired your riches and power and have brought gold and silver into your treasuries; by your great wisdom and by your trade you have increased your riches and power. **And your heart is proud and arrogant because of your wealth.**

"Therefore thus says the Lord God, 'Because you have imagined your mind [to be] like the mind of God [having thoughts and plans like God Himself], [Obadiah. 3] therefore, behold, I will bring strangers (Babylonians) upon you, the most ruthless and violent of the nations. And they will draw their swords against the beauty of your wisdom [O Tyre] and defile your splendor.

They will bring you down to the pit [of destruction], and you will die the death of all those who die .... Will you still say, "I am a god," in the presence of him who kills you?

But you are [only] a man [made of earth] and not God, *in the hands of those who wound and profane you.*

You will die the death of the uncircumcised [barbarian] by the hand of strangers, for I have spoken! Says the Lord God.""

———————————

3. This passage starts with God confronting the human leader of Tyre.

The Fall of Satan "The King of Tyre"

"Again the word of the LORD came to me, saying, 'Son of man, take up a dirge (funeral poem to be sung) for the king of Tyre[4] and say to him, "Thus says the Lord God, 'You had the full measure of perfection and the finishing touch [of completion], full of wisdom and perfect in beauty. You were in Eden, the garden of God. Every precious stone was your covering ....

You were the anointed cherub who covers and protects, and I placed you there.

You were on the holy mountain of God; you were blameless in your ways from the day you were created until unrighteousness and evil were found in you.

Through the abundance of your commerce you were internally filled with lawlessness and violence, and you sinned;

Therfore I have cast you out as a profane and unholy thing from the mountain of God ....'"

If you are interested in studying this subject further, be sure to read Ezekiel 26 and 27 to see more detail about the context of this passage.

I wanted you to see how far, how hard and why this very

---

4. God's understanding of the real culprit goes much deeper than Tyre's leader ever had a clue! **Notice that His biblical confrontation has now shifted from a human leader to the supernatural fallen angel, Satan!** At this time in history, he was apparently fallen and was manifesting as the evil territorial spirit over Tyre, deceiving their human leader into believing that he is a god. **Satan cost this man his eternal life. How does this relate to the US today?**

honored and blessed heavenly being fell and was cast out then; and, ultimately, will be thrown into the lake of fire to suffer for all eternity. Our God had created him as a cherub that covers. This phrase refers to the cherubim, highly honored heavenly beings positioned the closest to God. They cover the ark of His presence with their wings.

Satan maintained this position of great honor and perfection **until** he sinned through iniquities of pride, violence and his way of trading, probably evidenced with the destruction of Tyre because of their wickedness involving their huge international ungodly trade. This cherub being called the king of Tyre certainly alludes to his spiritual influence on the evil that caused Tyre's destruction by God. But Satan did, still does and will do far more than just help destroy Tyre and its leader; so we need to look much more deeply into his history and biblical prophecy to see the rest of his story.

**Let's First Look at His Names
to See How Far He Has Fallen.**

**Partial List of Biblical Names and
Descriptions of Satan NASB**

- *Satan, the great dragon, the serpent of old, the devil, who deceives the whole world*[5]
- *Accuser*[6]

---

5. Revelation 12:9
6. Revelation 12:10

- *Ruler of the demons[7]*
- *The tempter[8]*
- *The evil one[9]*
- *The enemy[10]*
- *Murderer from the beginning, the liar and father of lies[11]*
- *Your adversary, the devil, roaring lion, seeking someone to devour.[12]*
- *The god of this age who blinds minds[13]*

Satan, the thief, comes only to steal, kill, and destroy; but our LORD came and died on the cross for us so that we might have life and have it more abundantly.[14]

Satan, Kosmokrator, a Fallen Cherubim Angel, is Allowed to Rule Over Evil and Deceives Humans for this Age Only.

He will not be allowed to attack, deceive, torture or even harm humans forever. His eternal destiny is in the lake of fire, and that time is determined by God alone. Please don't let Satan deceive you and take you with him into eternal punishment. Jesus died so you could be with Him in

---

7. Matthew 9:34
8. Matthew 4:3
9. I John 5:19
10. Matthew 13:19
11. John 8:44
12. I Peter 5:8
13. 2 Corinthians 4:3-4, Prophecy Study Bible
14. John 10:10

Heaven forever. Eternal punishment was never meant for any human, but most will choose that hellish destiny!

After this age, Satan is bound for 1000 years! Listen to the details:[15] *"Then I saw an angel coming down from heaven, holding the key of the abyss and a great chain in his hand. And he laid hold of the* **dragon,** *the* **serpent of old,** *who is the* **devil** *and* **Satan,** *and bound him for a thousand years; and he threw him into the abyss, and shut it and sealed it over him,* **so that he would not deceive the nations any longer, until the thousand years were completed; after these things he must be released for a short time."**

Here is how Satan's rebellion against God ends: *"When the thousand years are completed, Satan will be released from his prison, and will come out to deceive the nations which are in the four corners of the earth,* **Gog and Magog, to gather them together for the war;** *the number of them is like the sand of the seashore. And they came up on the broad plain of the earth and* **surrounded the camp of the saints and the beloved city,** *and fire came down from heaven and devoured them. And the devil who deceived them was thrown into the lake of fire and brimstone, where the beast and the false prophet are also; and they will be tormented day and night forever and ever."*[16]

Hallelujah!

---

15. Revelation 20:1-3
16. Revelation 20:7-10 NASB

QUEEN OF HEAVEN

- **Second Wicked Leader of the Kingdom of Darkness**
- **Babylon the Great**[17]
- **Mother of Harlots**[18]
- **Queen of Heaven**[19]
- **The Queen of Heaven Is Responsible for <u>All</u> the Slain on the Earth**[20]

As we learned in Chapter 4, the second member of the satanic trinity is called **Mystery Babylon,**[21] and also **Babylon the Great, the Great Harlot,**[22] **the Mother of Harlots,**[23] **the Queen of Heaven** and many other names in various languages, like **Ishtar Ashtoreth** and **Astarte**. All these names make our understanding very complicated and confusing. Help us, Holy Spirit! Before we dig even more deeply into her strategies, let me remind you of the **universal magnitude** of her success in her deceptive wickedness and her ultimate hopes and plans for you and me and every other human on earth!

---

17. Babylon the Great: Revelation 17:5, 18:2
18. Mother of Harlots: Revelation 17:5
19. Queen of heaven: Jeremiah 7:18, 44:17,18,19,2
20. Queen of heaven: Revelation 18:24
21. Mystery Babylon: Revelation 17:
22. The great harlot
23. Mother of Harlots: Revelation 17:5

Revelation 18:24 Amplified Study Bible

"And in Babylon was found the blood of prophets and of saints (God's people) and of <u>all</u> those who have been slaughtered on the earth."

Please understand the magnitude of this evil. **This spirit, Mystery Babylon, is responsible for <u>all</u> the slain in the earth – <u>ALL</u>!**

Revelation 17:18 Amplified Study Bible

"The woman whom you saw is the great city, which reigns over and dominates and controls the kings and the political leaders of the earth."

The literal meaning of the word translated "reigns" is "has a kingdom," so this passage is saying that **there is a very high-level wicked spirit that somehow characterizes this great city and has a supernatural wicked kingdom that rules over the evil kings and political leaders of the whole earth.**

As we read passages like Revelation 17 and 18, it becomes very clear **how she gains this incredible control** – obviously through **worship of her as a false god,**[24] but much

---

24. Such as many in the Catholic Church do when they believe they have to go through Mary to get to God. In this theology, the precious human woman chosen to be the mother of the Son of God is replaced by the Queen of Heaven spirit and worshiped as the one they must go through to connect with God. This is a horrible, totally unbiblical heresy.

more cleverly and mostly undetected, <u>she primarily captures her prey through illicit sexual behavior "with her."</u> Of course, <u>almost nobody realizes that their immoral sexual harlotry with the opposite sex, homosexuality or even bestiality is also and primarily having sex with a very evil spirit, especially when it involves masturbation and fantasy!</u>

But this passage and many others make this reality quite clear!! **This is why <u>harlotry is repeatedly listed as one of the iniquities that can keep us out of heaven if we do not truly repent! God is not going to invite this spirit into heaven with any of us! We must be delivered first! Let me make something crystal clear: a child who is molested or a person who is raped is NEVER guilty of harlotry. But, if the spirit of harlotry that came into an innocent person later motivates them to voluntarily choose to commit sexual sin, that is their choice and they must take responsibility to repent of their sin, break the soul ties with that person or people and be delivered from that spirit.</u>**

Isaiah 47:10-11 NASB

Exposing this spirit, Isaiah says this about the reason that almost nobody connects his or her sexual sin with this spirit or understands the ultimate horrible eternal danger of this kind of behavioral iniquity. After all, isn't almost everybody operating in this behavior? It's no big deal, is it?

In this passage, Isaiah warns us about the spirit of harlotry and he warns the spirit herself! Listen!

"You felt secure in your wickedness and said, 'No one sees me.'"

"Your wisdom and your knowledge, they have deluded you; for you have said in your heart, 'I am, and there is no one besides me.' But evil will come upon you which you will not know how to charm away; and disaster will fall on you for which you cannot atone; and destruction about which you do not know will come on you suddenly."

We must take a long, hard look at this spirit and her huge influence and control on our country, the world and most critically and horrifyingly, ourselves!

<u>The danger of this wicked spirit seems to me to be even more frightening than that of Satan himself, because she is responsible for ALL the slain in the earth and we are all clueless about her until the LORD exposes her to us!</u>

<u>I had to be delivered from this spirit of harlotry as an adult because it came into me during the satanic ritual abuse and pedophilia I experienced as a young child. I was dissociated from those memories until I was much older. I had been a deliverance minister for years before I was spiritually and emotionally ready to face the reality of this hell I had lived from birth to probably 12.</u>

Please understand, without my having to share the absolutely hideous and horribly gory details of satanic ritual abuse or pedophilia, that everyone who goes through this could easily face a total emotional, mental, physical and spiritual breakdown and end up in an institution or on legal or illegal drugs to try and deal with the horror.[25] **Har-lotry is a spiritual issue and can <u>only</u> be resolved by Holy Spirit deliverance and the breaking of soul ties!**

I remember very little of my life before the age of about 12 because of the mercy of God. I have primarily remembered the hell in the context of God's supernatural healing when He showed up in the memory and ultimately transformed it into deliverance and safety in and with Him. **Only God can heal intimate encounters with hell so that he redefines everything that happened into supernatural escape into permanent safety and perfect love with Him!** So, the timing and ways that God reveals memories that are dissociated from a victim's conscious mind must be God-led 100%. Most of my deliverance from satanic ritual abuse and pedophilia have been private times with just God and me.

After the victim has been freed from hellish traumas and places of captivity, the next step in the process is for God to integrate the dissociated parts with the conscious part. Then the newly whole person can move toward shalom peace and safety in his or her deepest consciousness. It is a process I have experienced many, many times and am still experiencing whenever He knows I am ready. He will probably make sure that we victims never remember some hellish horrors! He is the Deliverer, Healer and also Perfect Love.

---

25. **Drugs and alcohol are just another way to get into an altered state of consciousness that connects you to evil spirits. Drugs are never the way out, but just another way into hellish bondage with evil spirits.**

In my conscious mind, I had no idea about the hell of my childhood until <u>Father God revealed the first horrid Satanic ritual memory to me in a terrifying flash-back!</u> It was His perfect timing and I was in the safe atmosphere He planned, surrounded by a small group of women who had also been through Satanic ritual abuse. The ministry leaders had deliberately placed me with them, in case God wanted to reveal something to me in that safe ministry setting!

But I still had no understanding, nor was I free from the spirit's influence on me until I was delivered! Remembering is not deliverance! It takes a God-encounter as He redefines the memory to empower you to be delivered. Only He can do that kind of miracle, but He can and will if you let Him. From that moment on, your memory has a happy ending – a God encounter!

Don't you be afraid. God has the perfect time, place and the helpers you need all planned for you, personally. He will make it safe for you to remember and be delivered from whatever binds you. Only He knows what you need to be healed from your hell planned by Satan. <u>You are on God's "appointment book!"</u>

We can trust our God to know when we are ready to face hellish memories like this, if they are a part of our life's history.

Let me be sure that you understand that if you have been sexually abused as a child or raped as an adult, you will have to break soul ties and be delivered from transmitted sexual spirits like the spirit of harlotry to be free, just like you would have to be treated for a sexually transmitted disease, no matter how those spirits or diseases got into you. <u>You must be delivered to be set free!</u>

<u>But if we willfully participated in sexual sin, we are guilty and must also repent of harlotry or whatever the sin was. You must not try to take these spirits into heaven with you.</u> The blood of Jesus has paid in full for all harlotry, even if we were the pedophile or satanist who raped and sacrificed victims! He only requires that we truly repent, for He has totally paid for all sin for all time and for every single human being world-wide. Once we repent, the spirit of harlotry can and must be cast out. Don't forget related spirits like lying spirits, spirits of betrayal and covenant breaking.

<u>There are multiple passages in the Bible that list iniquitous lifestyles that will keep a person out of heaven if not repented of, but I have never heard a sermon on them, although I have been in church for 85 years!</u>

<u>All of these passages below and many more list dire warnings about the eternal consequences of practicing the different kinds of harlotrous sins!</u> My goal here is not to make anyone feel shame or condemnation, but to save souls eternally. So, let's take a deep dive into the Word of God to see what He says about the dangers of our potential sins with this evil spirit, no matter whether we have a clue about her or not. We surely cannot afford to be ignorant about these warnings any longer. Please listen. Repent, break soul ties with the people and cast out the spirit of harlotry and any other spirits like lust or homo-

sexuality, in the name of Jesus, if you need to. Then help me to spread these little-known biblical warnings. And make sure that each person you warn knows he can repent, be delivered and be forgiven totally. Jesus died for all of our sins.

I Corinthians 6:9-10 NASB

"Or do you not know that <u>the unrighteous will not inherit the kingdom of God?</u>

Do not be deceived; **neither fornicators,** *nor idolators, nor* **adulterers,** *nor* **effeminate,** *nor* **homosexuals,** *nor thieves nor the covetous, nor drunkards, nor revilers nor swindlers,* **will inherit the kingdom of God.** <u>Such were some of you, but you were washed, but you were sanctified, but you were justified in the name of the Lord Jesus Christ and in the Spirit of our God."</u>

Galatians 5:19-25 NASB

"... the deeds of the flesh are ... immorality, impurity, sensuality, idolatry, sorcery, enmities, strife, jealousy, outbursts of anger, disputes, dissensions, factions, envying, drunkenness, carousing, and things like these, of which I forewarn you, just as I have forewarned you, that <u>those who practice such things will not inherit the kingdom of God.</u>

But the fruit of the Spirit is love, joy, peace, patience, kindness, goodness, faithfulness, gentleness, self-control; against such things there is no law. Now <u>those who belong to Christ Jesus have crucified the flesh with its passions and desires. If we live by the Spirit, let us also walk by the Spirit,"</u>

Ephesians 5:1-11 NASB

*"... be imitators of God, as beloved children ... and walk in love.... But **immorality** or any impurity or greed **must not even be** named among you ... For you know with certainty, that <u>no immoral or impure person or covetous man, who is an idolater, has an inheritance in the kingdom of Christ and God.</u>*

Let no one deceive you with empty words, for because of these things the wrath of God comes upon the sons of disobedience, Therefore, do not be partakers with them; for <u>you were formerly darkness, but now you are Light in the Lord; walk as children of Light (for the fruit of the Light consists in all goodness and righteousness and truth), trying to learn what is pleasing to the Lord.</u>

<u>Do not participate in the unfruitful deeds of darkness, but instead, even expose them; for it is disgraceful even to speak of the things which are done by them in secret. But all things become visible when they are exposed by the light, for everything that becomes visible is light."</u>

Revelation 22:12-17 NASB

"Behold, I am coming quickly (better translation "suddenly"), and My reward is with Me, to render to every man according to what he has done. I am the Alpha and the Omega, the first and the last, the beginning and the end.

Blessed are those who wash their robes, so that they may have the right to the tree of life, and may enter by the gates into the city.

<u>Outside</u> are the dogs and the sorcerers and <u>the immoral persons</u> and the murderers and the idolaters and <u>everyone who loves and practices lying.</u>

I, Jesus, have sent my angel to testify to you these things for the churches...

The Spirit and the bride say, 'Come.' And let the one who hears say, 'Come.' And let the one who is thirsty come; let the one who wishes take the water of life without cost."

<u>Let me quote a few passages to make sure we all get the point of this little understood reality about sexual immorality clearly, without a shadow of a doubt! The deception about harlotry is so great that I want to be sure that no reader of my book misunderstands what God's Word says on the subject or how badly He wants us all to repent and spend eternity with Him.</u> He wants that so badly that He became a man and died on the cruel cross to save every one of us from our iniquities that would disqualify us from eternity with Him.

Revelation 17:1-2 NASB

"Then one of the seven angels ... spoke with me, saying, <u>'Come here, I will show you the judgment of the great harlot ... with whom the kings of the earth committed acts of immorality, and those who dwell on the earth were made drunk with the wine of her immorality.'</u>"

Revelation 18:3,9-10 NASB

*"For **all the nations** have drunk of the wine of the **passion of her immorality**, and <u>the kings of the earth have committed acts of immorality with her</u>, and the **merchants of the earth** have become rich by the wealth of **her sensuality**.*

*And the <u>kings of the earth, who committed acts of immorality and lived sensuously with her</u>, will weep and lament over her when they see the smoke of her burning, standing at a distance because of the **fear of her torment**, saying, 'Woe, woe, the great city, Babylon, the strong city! For in one hour your judgment has come.'"*

<u>If you are guilty of this sin of harlotry, this would be a perfect time to repent, because the blood of Jesus was shed so you can be forgiven and free right now. There will never be a better time to wash all this guilt away by the blood of Jesus and be all new and clean.</u>

I don't know about you, but all this reality makes me run from sexual sin with more horror than anything I have ever been tempted to participate in! Can you imagine how hideous and terrifying this **spiritual hag** truly is?

<u>Surely, none of us want to see her hideous face waiting for us to claim us to be destined to spend eternity with her in her eternal torment from judgment day, forever! Understand that this is her whole wicked eternal purpose: she does not want to suffer alone, but wickedly wants to take us all with her!</u>

BUT GOD!!!

Galatians 5:1, 22-23

"It was for freedom that Christ set us free ...."

Once we have repented and fled from the Spirit of Harlotry, there should be no more shame and no more guilt! Listen to David, who certainly had to repent of this iniquity of harlotry and much more. Let's hear his experience of forgiveness from Father God.

Psalms 103:10-13 NASB

*"He has not dealt with us according to our sins, nor rewarded us according to our iniquities. For **as high as the heavens are above the earth, so great is His lovingkindness toward those who fear Him. As far as the east is from the west, so far has He removed our transgressions from us.** As a father has compassion on his children, so the Lord has compassion on those who fear Him."*

Please let this be the moment you receive the full cleansing and forgiveness Jesus died for you to experience from all sexual iniquity.

And **then pray for the breaking of every soul tie to every person you ever had sex with or were sexually abused by.** If you do this, you will be amazed at the freedom you experience, and the prayer is not hard or complicated, although it may take some time, depending on your situation. But the difference you feel will be awesome and eternally critical.

The blood of Jesus is enough to wipe this whole history from God's records in heaven, even if you have been a satanic ritual abuse victim from birth or a victim of a pedophile ring, like I was. Voluntary and involuntary sexual iniquities will be eternally erased by the blood of Jesus, and you can be a pure, chaste virgin, male or female, in God's eyes! When I prayed prayers like these, I was so amazed at the freedom I felt and how clean I knew I was in God's eyes. Please take the time to thoroughly let Him cleanse you. I promise that you will never regret it.

Allow me to include a list of sample prayers you can use as models to break every ungodly soul tie and cleanse your body, soul and spirit from defilement, eternally:

Do not do any of this repentance generically, but stay with each issue that applies to you until you have given Holy Spirit time to bring every single individual name of every person you were involved in sexual immorality with mentally or physically, voluntarily or involuntarily, before you leave that issue. Generic or theoretic repentance is no repentance at all! Take as long as it takes to get totally free. You will never regret it, I promise. Ask Holy Spirit to not let you forget one single issue or person, so that you can be totally free. He is faithful. BE SURE THAT YOU READ THIS WHOLE LIST FIRST BEFORE YOU START REPENTING SO YOU UNDERSTAND THE PROCESS.

- Go to a totally private place when you have plenty of time, totally alone with God, with no phone or human distractions. Be sure that you have pen and paper and your Bible, in case God wants you to look something up.

- Ask the LORD to bring to your mind every ungodly sexual use of your body and write them down so that you can repent. Use the prayers below as models. **At this point, you are just making a list, not repenting yet**.
- Next, go back over each encounter on your list and thoroughly repent for every detail the LORD brings to your mind. Then break the soul ties with each person.
- Breaking soul ties is not complicated. In the name of Jesus you can ask the Lord to break all ungodly soul ties with the person you had an ungodly relationship with and He will do what you ask. You will be amazed at the miraculous results of those simple prayers. He will truly set you free.
- **See the detailed list of sample prayers below**.
- After you are totally through repenting and breaking soul ties, cast out the spirits such as harlotry, lust, adultery, lying, homosexuality, lesbianism, masturbation, etc. Then ask the LORD to fill you afresh with the Holy Spirit. **When you are totally finished praying through this list in great detail, I recommend that you burn the list as a prophetic act that all this hell and guilt is now erased from your books in heaven and eternally under Jesus' blood. You will never have to answer for any of it again.**
- **If you are or were married at the time of these sexual sins, including masturbation and fantasy, and you really want to be free and forgiven by God, you must confess and repent in fullness to**

the person you are or were in marital covenant with. Breaking a marriage covenant is a very serious iniquitous sin in God's eyes and should be in ours, too. Without confession to the person you are or were in covenant with, you have not truly repented! If the other person is remarried, you must get direction from God about how to deal with this issue. You could cause serious problems. Obey Him completely.

- **Starting with childhood, let me give you some sample prayers that might help you.**
- Example: The list might start with "playing doctor" as a child, so you could pray, "Father, I repent for playing doctor with Johnny and ask you to forgive and cleanse me and break all ungodly soul ties with him."
- Break the soul ties as you go, but don't cast out the spirits until you are finished with all the repentance.
- Example: "Father, I repent for allowing myself to be touched inappropriately by Jimmy, or for touching Jimmy inappropriately. Please forgive me and break those soul ties with him and set me free."
- Example: "Oh Father, I am seeing myself being inappropriately touched by my uncle Charlie when I was a little girl. I feel dirty and guilty, even though I didn't understand what was happening or what I should do. Please forgive me for not telling anyone. I just felt terrified and bad. I choose to forgive him and cry out for you to break

all ungodly soul ties with him in the name of Jesus and by the power of His blood. Thank You, LORD, for cleansing me."

- Example: "Oh Father, now I feel so dirty and guilty, because I know I am totally guilty for the things I am remembering. I chose to act like a harlot and participate with my boyfriend in sexual behavior I knew was wrong as a teenager. Please forgive me and break all soul ties with Bill and set me free from that guilt and bondage to him. Thank You that Your blood is enough to cleanse me like a pure chaste virgin from that evil I chose to participate in."

- Example: "Oh Father, I chose to totally rebel against you and live with my boyfriend Jack as though we were married. Please forgive me and break all the ungodly soul ties from all that time of sinful living. I thank You that Your blood sacrifice was enough to totally cleanse all my filth from that relationship and make me whole and clean again."

- Example: "Oh Father, I am so guilty. I have been unfaithful to my wife with a coworker, It was so easy because we traveled together out of town for years on business. I got by with years of adultery, but I know I will stand before You and answer for every single act of harlotry. Please forgive me and break all soul ties with Mary. Help me genuinely totally repent to my wife and family, no matter the cost."

- Example: "Oh Father, when I was a little girl in Grade School and even a young teenager, I had some very demonized teachers who taught the whole class that we could choose what sex we were supposed to be! I know now what a lie that was, but I was too young then to know better. They were so sneaky and evil that we were programmed to keep what was going on from our parents until it was too late. This went on for years and I was secretly given hormones and treatments that have horribly changed me. Now I know how wrong this was, but it seems too late. I have seriously considered suicide, but I believe that You love me and don't want that for me. I also believe in miracles! Help me, Lord! You are the only one who can. Please! I break all soul ties with those evil people who want to destroy my identity as a girl and all soul ties with the false identity they put on me as a boy. I cast out every demonic spirit involved, in the name of Jesus. I am who You created me to be, a girl. I believe that You can do anything, so I am crying out to You for my true identity and healing."

- Example: "Oh LORD, I am such a mess that I have even been suicidal as I have faced the level of bondage and sin I have been trapped in as a lesbian (homosexual). I do not even truly understand what it means to be a woman. (man). I have been brainwashed, sexually abused as a child by men (women) and acted out most of my life as a result. Only You can understand my pain and confusion and deliver me from my sin and cleanse my body, soul and spirit to sexually live normally.

But I believe that You can and will. I now start by breaking all soul ties with every partner of every ungodly lesbian (homosexual) relationship and everyone who sexually abused or acted out with me. Please set me free from every human soul tie and every evil spirit I have willingly or forcibly ever connected with. Set me free and restore me by the blood of Jesus to be the person and the sex You created me to be. And then set me on the path to total healing and restoration. I will take the time to break soul ties and repent for each individual ungodly relationship or contact I ever had. Please don't let me forget anyone, so that I can be totally free. Thank You, LORD, because I know that only You can do this miracle for me. I fully trust You to set me free and restore me to who You created me to be. Thank You, LORD.

- Example: "Lord, much of my sexual acting out has been through masturbation and fantasy. I suppose that this ungodly sexual awakening in me happened by some childhood abuse, but I do not remember it, if it happened. I was exposed to pornography very young and immoral sexual TV and internet pictures. I guess my life could have been defiled that way and I could have been led into masturbation at this young age? I now know that what I thought was safe and not evil like real harlotry with people was actually sex with evil spirits who seduced me into masturbation, especially the wicked Spirit of Harlotry! I'm just now feeling dirty and beginning to understand a little about how evil and dangerous my behavior is. I have never confessed this to anyone. So, I now cry out to You to break all my soul ties to the Spirit of Harlotry and any other sexual evil spirit, or any real person I ever fantasized about. Please help me to thoroughly deal with my sin and never participate in this wicked and dangerous behavior again. (If you have participated in this sexual behavior, you have soul ties with the Queen of Heaven, Mystery Babylon that you must break. If you are a married man or woman, you have passed these spirits to your spouse when you had sex with her (him) and must repent to her or him. You should also warn them of the necessity for them and you to break the soul ties with the Harlot and other sexual spirits you have opened them up to and cast out the spirits from your lives in order for both of you to be set free. Also ask for forgiveness for the sin and betrayal of harlotry. Ask the LORD to help you replace every counterfeit with perfect love from Father for Him, yourself and others, with no more harlotry, ever.)

- If you have faithfully, to the best of your ability, completed this section of repentance and breaking soul ties, you should feel and be cleaner than you have ever been before and closer to your LORD and your spouse, if you are married.

- Don't forget to cast out all the spirits involved and ask that Holy Spirit fill you. If you are intimidated by this step, ask the LORD to help you connect with a Spirit-filled deliverance minister who can help you. Warning: Do not go to a church who does not believe in deliverance, such as most non-charismatic denominations such as Baptist, Methodist, Presbyterian, etc. Do not allow any unbeliever in the supernatural talk you out of your freedom.

- Please understand that if you have just repented to your spouse for iniquities she or he had no idea of, you cannot control their response. They will have to process this new reality and decide whether or not to forgive you and trust you and stay with you. If you have broken the marriage covenant, they have biblical grounds for divorce. Give them time, space and understanding, processing their behavior and response by facing how you would be feeling, reacting, processing and determining your future with them if they had just repented to you for the same iniquities and betrayal you confessed to them. Give them time and space with no pressure or condemnation, no matter how angry or unforgiving they are. Their decisions about how to react are totally their own and you must give them grace. Sin can be devastatingly expensive. It may even cost you your family and half or more of everything you own. If so, move on with God as a truly repentant child and never turn back to harlotry. Pay the just price for your sin and learn the lesson well. You have a promise that God will forgive you if your repentance is sincere, but with humans, there is no such guarantee. After all, you have willfully destroyed someone else's life and family to satisfy your lust and harlotry! Somebody will have to pay! Jesus already did, but human covenant keepers may decide to pay, too and forgive – or not! If they decide to carry the pain you caused forever and stay with you, never take this gift of love lightly and never betray them again. Don't ever forget that we will all stand before God and answer for every unforgiven sin. None of us want to have to pay for what we owe. Jesus already did. But there will always be consequences because other people are always involved when we sin sexually.

- Also understand that when you opened yourself up sexually to another person, you received all their generational and personal evil spirits plus those of everyone they ever had sex with. If you are married, were married when you committed adultery or ever marry in the future, you pass these spirits on to your spouse. To be free, you must repent, and you both must go through extensive deliverance.

If you are a pure, chaste virgin and one who has kept your whole life and marriage undefiled, praise God for you. May you always remain pure and be eternally blessed and rewarded for your obedience. Please allow Father to use you to help others overcome every plan of the Harlot for their life.

ANTICHRIST

Third Wicked Leader of the Kingdom of Darkness
The Antichrist, also Known as the Beast
Biblical Revelation

The Antichrist is the third member of the Kingdom of Darkness, opposing the Kingdom of our God, along with Satan and Mystery Babylon, the Queen of Heaven. This wicked being, in my opinion, is very likely alive today! He has to wait for his time to be satanically empowered through possession.[26] Only then, his resulting diabolical power will totally enable him to rule the whole world for evil. What he probably does not know is that he will only be allowed by God to manifest his wickedness for a set time, 7 years to be exact. His time on earth is all about our God allowing every man to freely choose eternal life with Him or eternal hell of punishment with evil men and the horrid fallen angels.

Jesus' Bride will not be a harlot, but a true lover of Father, His Son Yeshua (Jesus) and Holy Spirit. And nobody will ever deceive God about whether anyone is His son, Yeshua's true Bride or a harlot. **The Bride has a deep and intimate love relationship with her Bridegroom. Tragically, the human harlot also has a deep and intimate relationship with the Spirit of Harlotry, Mystery Babylon herself. But he or she is totally deceived through sexual deception and has no idea that the sexual thrill is**

---

26. Revelation 13:1-9

coming from the hideous Hag Harlotry Spirit and not the beauty or handsome lover fantasized about. This realization will only come with the horrifying meeting of their true lover, the Hag, in hell's eternal torment! What a shocking awakening every harlot has ahead of him or her! But the worst shock is that this hellish awakening is forever! The human harlot who never repents will never know true love because it only comes from God!

But we still get to decide our eternal fate. Seriously face the question: Which category do you fit into right this moment - harlot or Bride of Christ? There are only two choices!

This war for eternal souls is escalating like never before, as the time of the Antichrist rapidly approaches. Together, this false trinity certainly hopes and probably expects to win the final battle for humanity and the whole earth. They plan to defeat YHWH Elohim, the one and only true God, and steal mankind and earth from Him. Tragically, in one way, numerically, there is reality in their hope! The majority of God's creation will choose hell! The Bible says,

"Enter through the narrow gate. For wide is the gate and broad and easy to travel is the path that leads the way to destruction and eternal loss, and there are many who enter through it. But small is the gate and narrow and difficult to travel is the path that leads to [everlasting] life, and there are few who find it." 27

---

27. Matthew 7:13-14 Amplified Study Bible

The question is "Who will choose eternity with God and who will choose hell with Satan and his kingdom? **<u>Each person has been given a free will to choose his fate because God wants true lovers of Him. Love that is not voluntary is no love at all.</u>** So, if you are wavering in any way about your commitment to God, listen extra carefully! Understand the critical importance of discerning the counterfeit and the times.

Also understand that there is a **spirit of antichrist**[28] that manifests in many diabolical ways world-wide and deceives many through all the ages, but also **a specific Antichrist Entity who shows up on the world stage in the end times at the beginning of the seven-year Tribulation.**[29] **He is part of the False Trinity who counterfeits the true Trinity in the last days on earth before the Millenium. I am now unveiling this wicked one, biblically revealed, particularly in the book of Revelation.**

Meet the Antichrist (the Beast)

Revelation 13:1-2 Amplified Study Bible

"And the <u>dragon (Satan)</u> stood on the shore of the sea. ....

Then I saw a [vicious] <u>beast</u> coming up out of the sea .... And <u>the dragon gave him his power and his throne and great authority.</u>

---

28. I John 2:18-24
29. Revelation 6:2

So, Satan possesses Antichrist and sets him up in his position and authority in this evil kingdom on earth for 7 years.

In the book of Revelation, we see the introduction of this deceiving Antichrist riding in on his white horse in the disguise of the supernatural Messiah of the Jews and the awe-inspiring supernatural leader of everyone else who will believe his counterfeit.[30] I was listening today to the godless things going on in Israel and wondering just how close we are to this climatic time! Their deception is getting really scary! Thank God that true believers in Jesus are removed from the earth before the full - blown rule of the Antichrist and the wrath of God hits.[31]

At that time, pure evil will begin to take center stage on the earth! Antichrist is able to manifest his façade because most who are left on earth after the rapture will be easily deceived. This counterfeit is particularly targeting Israel, God's chosen people, and they have already set themselves up for deception by crucifying their true Messiah, Yeshua (Jesus).

However, the Bible also records that many will wake up at this point and remember the gospel they rejected. They will repent and believe. This, of course, will save their eternal lives, but they will have to go through part of the wrath of God never intended for them. Then they

---

30. Revelation 6:1-2
31. I Thessalonians 5:9-11

will join those who went up to be with the LORD in the rapture. Tragically, many will suffer martyrdom.[32]

As we just read, the Bible reveals this Antichrist as **the beast**[33] who is possessed by Satan himself.

"All who dwell on the earth will worship him, everyone whose name has not been written from the foundation of the world in the book of life of the Lamb."[34]

Why in the world would they fall for the Antichrist's deception? **Remember that Satan gives Antichrist his supernatural power! Not everything supernatural is God. All fallen angels and demons are supernatural** and for a price, even the price of eternal damnation in hell, will empower humans to get what they want. This is what is happening through the Antichrist in the beginning of his reign.

Many years ago, I was teaching the Book of Revelation and we decided to go and visit a Jewish Rabbi in Charleston, SC, where I lived at the time. Our purpose was to find out first hand what they expect from their Messiah. He graciously agreed to talk to us on the subject and I was absolutely shocked and horrified to hear his answers as we asked our questions. He described the biblical Antichrist to the letter! He said that their Messiah will be the most outstanding man, not God, who ever lived and he will make Israel the leading nation in the world! What a set up they

---

32. Revelation 7:9-17
33. Revelation 13:1-8
34. Revelation 13:8

will fall into! **They crucified their real Messiah and will fall for the Antichrist, but in YHWH's eternal love, mercy and covenant-keeping character, in mid-tribulation, He makes sure they wake up!**

In the beginning, the Antichrist draws everyone in through demonically empowered "miracles."

"I saw ... a fatal wound, but <u>his fatal wound was healed; and the entire earth followed after the beast</u> in amazement.

<u>They fell down and worshiped the dragon</u> because he gave his authority to the beast; <u>they also worshiped the beast</u>, saying, 'Who is like (as great as) the beast, and who is able to wage war against him?'"

"And the beast was given a mouth (the power of speech) uttering great things and arrogant and blasphemous words, and he was given freedom and authority to act and to do as he pleased for forty-two months (three and a half years). ...

And he opened his mouth to speak blasphemies (abusive speech, slander) against God, to blaspheme His name and His tabernacle, and those who live in heaven. He was also permitted to wage war against the saints (God's people) and overcome them, and <u>authority and power over every tribe and people and language and nation.</u>[35]

<u>All the inhabitants of the earth will fall down and worship him, everyone whose name has not been written since the</u>

---

35. Remember that everyone who was a true believer is already gone through the rapture, so these believers are the ones who have gotten saved since the rapture happened. They are new believers.

foundation of the world in the Book of Life of the Lamb, who has been slain [as a willing sacrifice].

If anyone has an ear, let him hear."[36]

During the Antichrist's rule, Revelation 6 chronicles the beginning of the true end time war between God and all who try to turn the humans left behind against Him. Again, **no human was ever destined to experience any of this – neither the wrath of God nor the punishment of His enemies, nor the wickedness of the Kingdom of Darkness. We see war, famine, death, over 1/3 of the earth population being killed by Death and Hades through the sword, famine, pestilence and wild beasts. From the enemy, we see martyrs slain because they testify the Word of God and even terror from God's wrath. This is definitely not a time when I want to be here. And this is just the time of the seals. It only gets worse through the end times Trumpets and the Bowls Judgements of the last 3 ½ years of the Tribulation.**

We believers are clearly told that we are not destined for wrath, but in the Book of Revelation during the 7 years of the Tribulation, in KJV version of the New Testament, the wrath of God is repeatedly chronicled 13 times![37] To me, this clearly points to the Pre-Tribulation Rapture timeframe.

---

36. Revelation 13
37. Revelation 6:16; 6:17; 11:18; 12:12; 14:19; 15:1; 15:7; 16:1; 16:19

FALSE PROPHET

Meet the One Who Helps Make It Even Worse – the Other Beast (False Prophet)

There is also a **second beast** manifesting during this time called the **false prophet. He leads the people to worship the Antichrist because he at least seems to have been supernaturally raised from death caused by a deadly head wound.**[38]

This false prophet is the one who is **empowered to kill**[39] **all who will not worship the image of the Antichrist.**[40]

Revelation 13:11-18 Amplified Study Bible

"Then <u>I saw another beast</u> rising up out of the earth....

<u>He exercises all the authority of the first beast in his presence</u>....

And <u>he makes the earth and those who inhabit it worship the first beast</u>....

<u>He performs great signs</u> ... even making fire fall from the sky ... and <u>he deceives</u> those [unconverted ones] ... because of the signs that he is given [by Satan] ...

<u>telling those who inhabit the earth to make an image of the beast</u> ....

---

38. Revelation 13:11-18
39. Revelation 13:15
40. Revelation 13:15

And he is given power to give breath to the image of the beast, so that the image of the beast will even [appear to] speak and cause those who do not bow down and worship the image of the beast to be put to death. ...."

"He also compels all ... to be given a mark on their right hand or on their forehead [signifying allegiance to the beast],.

... no one will be able to buy or sell, except the one who has the mark, either the name of the beast or the number of his name. Here is wisdom. Let the person who has enough insight calculate the number of the beast, for it is the [imperfect] number of a man, and his number is 666."

But that's not all the evil he does! He is also in charge of requiring all to take the mark of the beast or not be able to buy or sell![41]

The Antichrist is worshiped world-wide, and most shockingly, by Israel. For the first 3 1/2 years of his Tribulation reign, these Jews believe that Antichrist is their long-awaited Messiah.

At mid-Tribulation, the 3 ½ year mark, Antichrist goes into the Temple and declares himself God! With that blasphemy, Israel finally wakes up to his deception and, with God's help and protection, flees from his plans to destroy her.[42] Now the time begins for all Israel to be saved, with the help of the 144,000 Jewish evangelists consisting of 12,000 from each tribe.

---

41. Revelation 13:15-18
42. II Thessalonians 2:4

This wicked Antichrist beast, along with his false prophet, the second beast, are ultimately thrown into the lake of fire for eternal punishment. This happens right before the Millennial Reign of Jesus.[43]

At this time, Satan is not thrown into the lake of fire yet, but is bound up for the 1000 years Millennial Reign![44]

Follow me into the last chapter as we see how we can win this personal battle with Satan, the Spirit of Harlotry, the Antichrist and all evil spirits.

---

43. Revelation 19:20
44. Revelation 20:1-3, 7-9

6

HOW CAN I WIN?

Because YHWH our God is Love, the whole Bible starts and ends with His love story! But we still have some deep biblical mining to do to discover the full depth and complexity of God's love, especially as it manifests in the Book of Revelation. Let's review what we know.

In Genesis, the beginning of the Bible, the only true God creates the first man and woman in His own image and likeness and names them Adam and Eve. He designs them for perfect love with Him (Father, Son and Holy Spirit) and each other. He makes them to be fruitful and multiply, rule the earth under His authority and fill the earth with their offspring like you and me. We are also specifically created for eternal perfect love.

He places them in a beautiful garden in a world full of multiple varieties of plants and animals, all at perfect shalom peace with each other and their Creator. Everyone was created a vegetarian, so there was safety for all of creation on earth that we can't even imagine now. And **there is no death ever planned by God!**

But there was a usurper found in the garden with a very different plan - the serpent who had no authority on this newly created earth <u>until</u> Adam and Eve disobeyed God and gave their dominion to him.

This horrible, sinful fall of Adam and Eve from the perfect plan of our Creator God is beyond our understanding. Salvation from our forefathers' sins required the greatest act of love ever given. There was only one way for any man to ever be forgiven of sin and saved from eternal separation from God and His just punishment for sin.

Father God loved man and in His great mercy asked His only Son, Yeshua (Jesus), to be willing to become a lowly man, live a perfect sinless life on earth and die on a cruel cross as **the perfect sacrifice** for all mankind's sin. <u>Only</u> this incredible price could atone for man's sin in Father God's eyes!

And <u>only</u> those who would believe the facts that Jesus suffered and died for them personally, repent for their sins and surrender totally to Him as Savior and Lord would be saved from Hell. Then they could spend eternity with Him, God the Father, Holy Spirit, all the angels who did not fall with Satan and all believers of all time. Every human would have a choice to repent for his sins and believe in Jesus as his Savior and Lord or suffer for eternity, along with Satan, the Antichrist, the Queen of Heaven and all fallen angels, paying for his own sins in eternal hell fire.

There is no greater love story than Jesus' becoming a man and dying for you and me, but His story doesn't end there. Many believers in Jesus stop reading here and know nothing at all about the rest of the story - the End Times we are rapidly approaching! There is so much more to our story, so we must keep digging in the Bible through the last words in the Book of Revelation. There is even more of the love demonstrated on the cross to learn about and respond to. All true miners, keep digging for treasure, no matter how seemingly difficult the dig is. **We have Holy Spirit on board now because of the cross! He is our supernatural Teacher and Helper.**

In the very last book in the Bible, the Book of Revelation climaxes with His incredible eternal love story that no Hollywood script writer would ever even imagine!

If you have never read the back of the Book, you could never make this ending up either, not in a thousand years! And <u>you would never guess the eternal warning God gives to all who change one word of the Book of Revelation!</u>

None of us really know what He is about to do to show what perfect love truly looks like or the absolute horror

of the fate of His enemies.[1] The Bible is no soap opera! It is 100% reality, 100% justice, 100% perfect love and 0% codependency that He calls harlotry!

How can you and I win? Read the Book of Revelation and the whole Bible and contemplate how your own story will end based on what God says! Most people have watched thousands of TV shows and movies but very, very few have ever read the "punch lines" at the end of God's Word!

I guarantee you that the Book of Revelation is not boring. A glorious wedding with our Beloved follows the destruction of the Harlot, but instead of a Hollywood type honeymoon, He invites His Bride to join Him in His victory over all His and our enemies! Wow!

**Listen to Some of the Details about What Is Ahead.
The Church Age Is Completed with The Catching Away
(Rapture).**

At the perfect time,[2] the Church Age will be over. The Catching Away ("Rapture" in Latin Bible) will happen.

---

1. I find the warnings in Revelation 22:18-19 NASB absolutely terrifying for all who do not take the Book of Revelation and particularly this passage seriously. Listen carefully: *"I testify to everyone who hears the words of the prophecy of this book: if anyone adds to them, God shall add to him the plagues which are written in this book; and if anyone takes away from the words of the book of this prophecy, God shall take away his part from the tree of life and from the holy city, which are written in this book."* Do I have your attention now? Good! Let's keep reading and looking more deeply.
2. I Thessalonians 4:13 – 5:11

Our heavenly Bridegroom, Yeshua, the Son of God, will catch away His beloved Bride from the plan of hell itself who tries to take us all out. <u>Jesus' precious Bride is not destined for the wrath</u>[3] that is about to be unleashed by Jesus on all who will bow to the Antichrist and try to destroy His Bride. He will welcome us to live safely forever in perfect love with Him.

All children below the age of accountability (This age will vary, depending on maturity, but it is probably around 12.) will be caught up in the rapture. Just imagine the world-wide impact that event will cause!

The Tribulation for Seven Years

After the word-wide shock of the rapture, the greatest harvest ever will come during the Seals of the Great Tribulation. More than we can count from every tongue, tribe, people and nation will be saved![4] Think about what this catching away (rapture) of all the children world-wide will cause. I'm sure that the Fake News will have quite a tale to tell, but I don't believe they will convince a mother nursing her baby when he and her other three, five and seven-year-olds all disappeared before her eyes.

This harvest will also include millions who had thought they were saved until the rapture came, but they were left behind because they were actually just nominal Christians. Hallelujah for their eternal salvation, but all

---

3. I Thessalonians 5:9
4. Revelation 7:9-17

these will go through wrath never intended for God's children and probably martyrdom by the Antichrist.

Listen to some of the details about this horrible time when those left behind after the rapture have to face the Antichrist (beast) and the False Prophet (also called another beast) and their hellish plans. Revelation 13 gives us a lot of details, some prophetic and difficult to understand, but some very clear and terrifying. Let's look at a few of the details:

Antichrist (Beast) from Revelation 13

- He came up out of the sea.
- His power and authority came from Satan, the dragon.
- The whole earth followed him because he at least appeared to having been miraculously healed from a fatal head wound.
- He blasphemed God.
- He made war with the saints and overcame them and was given authority over every tribe, people, tongue and nation.
- Everyone on earth whose name is not written in the Lamb's book of life will worship the Antichrist.

False Prophet (Another Beast) from Revelation 13

- He came up out of the earth.
- He had two horns like a lamb, but spoke as a dragon.

- He exercises all the authority of the first beast in his presence, and makes people worship the antichrist.
- He deceives people with supernatural satanic power and signs.
- He makes fire come down out of heaven.
- He tells the people to build an image of the Antichrist beast.
- This image of the beast is demonically empowered to speak.
- Those who will not worship this image of the beast are killed.
- People are required to take the mark on their right hand or forehead, and whoever refuses will not be able to buy or sell.
- The number if the beast is 666.

Revelation 14:9-11

Wrath of God for Everyone Who Worships the Beast Delivered to Those Who Have Chosen to Receive the Mark.

A third angel cries out, "If anyone worships the beast and his image, and receives the mark on his forehead, or upon his hand, he will drink of the wine of the wrath of God, which is mixed in full strength in the cup of His anger; and he will be tormented with fire and brimstone in the presence of the holy angels and in the presence of the Lamb. And the smoke of their torment goes up forever and ever; and they have no rest day

<u>and night: those who worship his image, and whoever receives the mark of his name.</u>"

Revelation 14:12-13

But This is the Eternal Promise
To Those Who Keep the Commandments of God
During This Hellish Time

"Here is the perseverance of the saints who keep the commandments of God and their faith in Jesus.

And I heard a voice from heaven saying, 'Write, "Blessed are the dead who die in the Lord from now on!"' 'Yes,' says the Spirit, 'that <u>they may rest from their labors, for their deeds follow with them.</u>'

144,000 Thousand Jews

12,000 from each tribe, are sealed to be evangelists during the Tribulation.[5] But it will be time for Israel to face her Antichrist, having crucified her Savior and now believing that this most wicked of men is her Messiah for 3 1/2 years. At this point, he goes into the Temple and declares himself God and Israel is horrified. <u>Finally, all Israel alive at that time will flee, be protected from the Antichrist and finally be truly saved.</u>[6]

---

5. Revelation 7:4-8
6. Romans 11:26

Our Enemy, Responsible for All the Slain on the Earth,[7] Called the Harlot, Is Taken Out Permanently.

Revelation 19:1-3 NASB

... *"Hallelujah! Salvation and glory and power belong to our God; BECAUSE HIS JUDGMENTS ARE TRUE AND RIGHTEOUS; for He has judged the great harlot who was corrupting the earth with her immorality, and HE HAS AVENGED THE BLOOD OF HIS BONDSERVANTS ON HER." And a second time they said, "Hallelujah! <u>HER SMOKE RISES UP FOREVER AND EVER</u>."*

Then Comes the Glorious Marriage of Jesus and His Bride.

Revelation 19:7-8

... *"Let us rejoice and be glad and give the glory to Him; for <u>the marriage of the Lamb has come and His bride has made herself ready</u>." It was given to her to clothe herself in fine linen, bright and clean, for the fine linen is the righteous acts of the saints."*

Glory, Glory, Glory! Now Behold King Jesus Waging War on Every Enemy.

---

7. Revelation 18:24 NASB "And in her was found the blood of prophets and of saints and of **all who have been slain on the earth.**"

Revelation 19:11-13

... *"And I saw heaven opened, and behold, a white horse, and He who sat on it is called Faithful and True, and in righteousness He judges and wages war. His eyes are a flame of fire, and on His head are many diadems; and He has a name written on Him which no one knows except Himself. He is clothed with a robe dipped in blood, and His name is called, The Word of God."*

Look! Our Bridegroom Is Not Alone!

Revelation 19:14-16

"And the armies which are in heaven, clothed in fine linen white and clean, were following Him on white horses." (That would be His Warrior Bride)

"From His mouth comes a sharp sword, so that with it He may strike down the nations, and He will rule them with a rod of iron, and He treads the wine press of the fierce wrath of God the Almighty. And on His robe and on His thigh He has a name written, 'KING OF KINGS, AND LORD OF LORDS.'

Our LORD Wins Totally and Eternally!

Revelation 19:19-20:7

... *"And I saw the beast and the kings of the earth and their armies assembled to make war against Him who sat on the horse and against His army. And the <u>beast was seized and with</u>*

him the false prophet who performed the signs in his presence, by which he deceived those who had received the mark of the beast and those who worshiped his image; these two were thrown alive into the lake of fire which burns with brimstone."

"And the rest were killed with the sword which came from the mouth of Him who sat on the horse...."

"Then I saw an angel coming down from heaven, holding the key of the abyss and a great chain in his hand. And he laid hold of the dragon, the serpent of old, who is the devil and Satan, and bound him for a thousand years, and he threw him into the abyss, and shut it and sealed it over him, so that he would not deceive the nations any longer until the thousand years were completed;"

"... after these things he must be released for a short time."

I don't know about you, but I would say that Our Bridegroom's idea of a Honeymoon is certainly not going to be boring! For all who have chosen to give everything to Him, there is no end to our experiencing His love. What a way to start!

As we complete our study of our enemies who have tried to steal us, Jesus' Bride, from Him and rob us all of perfect eternal love, now it's time to take a truly close look at our own lives. Throughout all these centuries, every person has had to make the same choices Adam and Eve were required to make. **Where are you and I in our personal love story with YHWH?**

Jesus Clearly Answered our Question:
"How Can I Win?"

Matthew 22:36-49 NASB

"Teacher, which is the great commandment in the Law?

And He said to him, 'YOU SHALL LOVE THE LORD YOUR GOD WITH ALL YOUR HEART, AND WITH ALL YOUR SOUL, AND WITH ALL YOUR MIND.[8]

This is the great and foremost commandment,

the second is like it, 'YOU SHALL LOVE YOUR NEIGHBOR AS YOURSELF.'

On these two commandments depend the whole Law and the Prophets.' "

With a cursory reading, minus what we just read, this passage sounds good with no problem. But if you have just read this book and seriously looked at the wrath of God and its eternal consequences, you might realize that you need much more understanding about YHWH's perfect love!

Didn't we just read about an eternal Lake of Fire for his

---

8. *Deuteronomy 6:5-9 NASB "You shall love the LORD your God with all your heart and with all your soul and with all your might. These words, which I am commanding you today, shall be on your heart. You shall teach them to your sons and shall talk of them when you sit in your house and when you lie down walk by the ways when you lie down and when you rise up.... You shall write them on the doorposts of your house and on your gates."*

enemies? Surely that destiny for His enemies is not a manifestation of a loving God – or is it?

Let's think again??? If Heaven were full of satanists and pedophiles, could it possibly be heaven? Would it be safe? If harlots, pedophiles, robbers and wicked men were your next - door neighbors, would heaven be a place of eternal joy? So how do we understand God's judgment of His enemies and how can we win? What are we missing? Is it our understanding of both love and justice?

Have we been taught about what biblical love truly looks like, or have we been deceived by our old enemies, Satan and the harlot, and been taught codependency and misogyny instead of biblical love as the way of life God's people are supposed to live? Is this perverted marital and societal structure I just pictured practiced, even in the church? And is its toleration taught as biblical love?

LORD, there must be teaching in Your Word that most people never study, just like we haven't fully studied the Book of Revelation.

And if there is as much there on this subject as we have found in Revelation, so far, on other critical subjects, no wonder we don't know how to truly love the way You love. And no wonder our nation, marriages, families and whole lives are so ungodly and painful.

Holy Spirit, we are crying out for revelation in Your Word. And we miners are opening our Bibles as our treasure book, admitting that we have not dug deeply enough to find major life lessons that just might transform us and save our lives on this earth and in eternity. I have a feeling that we are in for some shocks as big as we just felt when we started studying the Book of Revelation. And we are still learning the magnitude of the battle against the One who is Perfect Love and all of us who love Him as His eternal Bride.

Maybe we still need to dig a whole lot more deeply in the Bible to know how we can win. Revelation is not easy to understand and we just faced some shocking facts about our deceptions about what love really is, so I suspect that we have a lot more to learn before we know how to win!

But we are ready for our deepest dig yet! Right, miners? How can we really love Yeshua like He loves us, and how can we love others as He does? Holy Spirit, teach us what the Word says about how to truly love.

I have written another book entitled "Agape Is Not Sloppy!" (Agape is the biblical Greek word for love.) This book covers what God taught me from His Word on this subject. Allow me to share a little of what I learned about the question, "How can I love different kinds of people?"

Have you been taught that you love everyone the same way? Isn't that the fair way? Aren't you just supposed to tolerate and forgive everyone's sin against you and bless them? Aren't you to cover up all the evil going on in your family and act like everyone is loving and wonderful and never tell family secrets, no matter how hellish and demonic they really are? Isn't that what love is?

If you are a wife being ignored, betrayed and verbally abused, aren't you just supposed to be submissive and suffer silently? Aren't you biblically promised that this is the way of guaranteeing that you will be loved and blessed by your husband and God? If you work hard enough and just change enough to please your husband, more than his other lovers, isn't that what love is? Is this way of submission not what you are to teach your children as the way of God? Men, are you supposed to just tolerate a cheating, lying, wicked wife with other lovers, acting just like I described above? Is that what forgiveness means?

Miners, let's do a little digging and see what diamonds in the rough the Bible, and particularly Psalms, Proverbs and I and II Corinthians put in our hands on this subject. We are trying to learn how to love different kinds of people biblically and be ready when Jesus comes for us. I'm now realizing that we all will probably have to shift some worldly and religious and even totally demonically inspired mindsets to really love like God loves.

A Short Synopsis of Biblical Instructions: How to Love of Different Kinds of People

The Wise Man

The Wise Man's Biblical Characteristics

- He understands the lovingkindness of God.[9]

---

9. Psalm 107:43

- He fears God and turns away from evil.[10]
- He is not wise in his own eyes.[11]
- If you wisely rebuke a wise man, he will love you.[12]
- He becomes yet wiser when he is given instruction.[13]

How Do You Biblically Love a Wise Man?

- You talk to him openly and honestly about anything you want to without fear that he will laugh at you or rage at you.[14]
- Know that he will truly hear you, so you can expect this relationship to be real and fulfilling. So, love him by being wise and understanding, too.[15]
- Listen to his wise counsel in strategizing for dangerous situations and seeking safety.[16]
- Reprove him when he needs correction and he will love you. A reproof enters more into a wise man than 100 stripes into a fool.[17]
- His tongue brings healing to you. Make sure that yours does the same for him.

---

10. Proverbs 14:16
11. Proverbs 26:12
12. Proverbs 9:8
13. Proverbs 9:9
14. Proverbs 29:9
15. Proverbs 1:5
16. Proverbs 24:6; 21:22
17. Proverbs 17:10

The Fool

The Fool's Biblical Characteristics

- The fool has said in his heart, "There is no God."[18]
- For My people are foolish. They know Me not. They are stupid children and have no understanding. They are shrewd to do evil. But to do good they do not know.[19]
- A fool always loses his temper. But a wise man holds it back.[20]
- A fool's lips bring strife. And his mouth calls for blows. A fool's mouth is his ruin. And his lips are the snare of his soul.[21]
- A man who commits adultery is a fool.

How to Biblically Love a Fool?

- Answer not a fool according to his folly, lest you, too, be like him.[22]
- Wisdom is too high for a fool. Speak not in the ears of a fool, for he will despise the wisdom of your words.[23]
- Love them. Don't join them!
- Like Abagail in the Bible, don't allow yourself to

---

18. Psalms 14:1
19. Jeremiah 4:22
20. Proverbs 29:11
21. Proverbs 18:6-7
22. Proverbs 26:4
23. Proverbs 24:7; 23:9

be the victim of their foolishness. Take things into your own hands, with God's direction, when necessary to protect yourself and household.[24]

- The Prodigal Son in the Bible was definitely a fool, wasting his life and fortune on loose and foolish living, to the point of near destruction. But it was his father's heart to restore to his son all he had thrown away and see him delivered by perfect love and grace. But this father was not a fool, so he wisely waited for his son to truly repent and come home changed **before** he restored him with lavish blessings.[25]

The Wicked Man

The Wicked Man's Biblical Characteristics

- They trip up other people's feet on purpose.[26]
- The mouth of the wicked conceals violence.[27]
- A city is torn down by the mouth of the wicked.
- There is no fear of God in the wicked.[28]
- Salvation is far from the wicked.[29]

---

24. I Samuel 25
25. Luke 15:11-32
26. Psalms 149:4
27. Proverbs 10:11
28. Proverbs 11:11
29. Psalms 119:155

How to Biblically Love the Wicked Man

- First, understand that wickedness is never from God, but strictly from the devil.
- Do not tolerate wickedness. It is deadly for all its victims.
- Remove the wicked man from among you until and unless he truly repents and is delivered.[30]
- If he repents, be willing, with extreme caution, to follow the LORD's specific direction to restore him to God.
- Whether or not he can or should be restored to those he has betrayed and harmed must be 100% Holy Spirit led. Codependency, which is actually harlotry, can have no place in these personal decisions by all who have been betrayed and devastated by these iniquities against them. Also, there must be anointed spiritual help, and an understanding and appropriate deliverance to deal with all open doors, especially relational and sexual open doors. You must understand that if you are having or have had sex with this newly repentant person, all the evil spirits he (she) has opened himself (herself) up to by his (her) sin already have access to you.

---

30. I Corinthians 5; II Corinthians 2:4—17. A member of the church was sleeping with his step mother and had to be removed from the church in order not to defile it. Paul had written these instructions to the church. Now he had repented, so Paul wrote to the church and counselled them to reinstate him into the church and forgive him so that he could move on in his faith.

- But he or she can be delivered and set free. It is not hopeless, but all the spirits who have been given access through his (her) sin must be cast out and he (she) must be filled by the Spirit so they do not return. He (she) will have to deal with both generational and personal iniquities and evil spirits of everyone he (she) has opened himself (herself) up to. It sounds complex because it is! That is why we are commanded to be faithful to one spouse for life. Do not enter back into an intimate relationship with the betrayer without dealing with all this supernatural baggage!

- Both you and your spouse will have to go through extensive deliverance and inner healing, breaking all the ungodly soul ties and sexual bondages that have resulted from their sin. You will even have to be delivered from generational iniquities of the bloodlines and other sex partners of every person he or she has exposed you and him (her) to. This is no small issue. And the results can be deadly for both the guilty and the innocent partner of such a marriage. Very few pastors have any understanding of these complications, and many just basically say, "Forgive and forget!!!" This advice is terribly unwise and ALWAYS ends in disaster for both the guilty and the innocent partner.

We Probably Are Much Closer to the Revelation of Jesus Christ than Anyone Knows!
Let's Make Sure We Are Ready!

Nobody Will Be Ready Who Has Not Studied Revelation!

Studying the Book of Revelation

I have been shocked as I have found out how few Christian leaders have even read the Book of Revelation, much less studied it! Yet **it is the only book in the Bible that promises a blessing if you read it! Listen:**

Revelation 1:3 Amplified Study Bible

"Blessed (happy, prosperous, to be admired) is he who reads and those who hear the words of the prophecy, and who keep the things which are written in it [heeding them and taking them to heart] ....

And it is the only book in the Bible that threatens you with a terrible curse if you change one word of it! Listen:

Revelation 22:18-19

"I testify and warn everyone who hears the words of the prophecy of this book [the predictions, consolations, and admonitions]: if anyone adds [anything] to them, God will add to him the plagues (afflictions, calamities) which are written in this book; [Deut. 4:2]

And if anyone takes away from or distorts the words of the book of this prophecy, God will take away [from that one] his share from the tree of life and from the holy city (new Jerusalem), which are written in this book."

In my opinion, these verses contain one of the most important warnings in the entire Bible, and it will affect probably millions of "Bible scholars," but <u>I have never heard this warning mentioned anywhere, never!!</u> I take it very seriously, very, very, very seriously! How about you? <u>Do you dare to say that the Book of Revelation is not relevant or change what it says? Not me!</u>

Other Repeated Terrifying Warnings

The enemy wants us to believe that we can habitually disobey God and live in any sinful lifestyle we wish and still spend eternity with God. <u>Just believing in Jesus does not save you from your sins. You must repent of your sins and give Him your whole life. If you read the Bible seriously at all, you rapidly learn that. The Bible repeats God's warnings over and over because He does not want any of us to go to hell when we could repent and believe and give our life to Yeshua (Jesus) and spend eternity with Him. He is requiring me to quote a number of these passages here to make sure that every reader hears His voice on the subject. If you have struggled or are struggling with any of the sins mentioned below and haven't truly repented, please cry out to God before it is too late and repent from your heart.</u>

The Very First Word Jesus Spoke When He Started His Ministry

Matthew 4:17 NASB

"From that time, Jesus began to preach and say, '<u>Repent</u>, for the kingdom of heaven is at hand.'"

<u>Take very serious note of how Jesus introduced the world to how to be saved from its sin. It was not just to believe in who He is!</u>

James 2:14, 17-20 NASB

"What use is it, my brethren, if a man says he has faith, but he has no works? Can that faith save him? ... faith, if it has no works, is dead ... You believe that God is one. You do well: <u>demons also believe, and shudder. But are you willing to recognize, you foolish fellow, that faith without works is useless?</u>"

<u>Study the Scriptures below and search your own heart. Be sure you are truly repentant of all these iniquities in your life and believe that Jesus is the true Son of God who died for your sins before you call yourself a born again Christian. It takes both repentance and belief to save you from hell fire. That is what the Bible teaches over and over and over. Please listen very carefully and understand that there are many more verses on the same subject. Our LORD does not want anyone to misunderstand what is necessary to truly be saved and spend eternity with Him.</u>

Galatians 5:13-24

"... you were called to freedom ... only do not turn your freedom into an opportunity for the flesh....

... walk by the Spirit and you will not carry out the desire of the flesh. For the flesh sets its desire against the Spirit, and the Spirit against the flesh; for these are in opposition against one another, so that you may not do the things that you please,

*... Now the **deeds of the flesh** are evident, which are **immorality**, impurity, sensuality, **idolatry**, sorcery, enmities, **strife, jealousy, outbursts of anger, dissensions, factions, envying, drunkenness,** carousing, and things like these,*

of which <u>I forewarn you, just as I have forewarned you that those who practice such things shall not inherit the kingdom of God.</u>

<u>But the fruit of the Spirit is love, joy, peace, patience, kindness, goodness, faithfulness, gentleness, self-control; against such things there is no law,</u>

<u>Now those who belong to Christ Jesus have crucified the flesh with its passions and desires."</u>

I Corinthians 6:9-11

"... do you not know that <u>the unrighteous will not inherit the kingdom of God?</u> Do not be deceived: <u>neither fornicators,</u> nor <u>idolaters,</u> nor <u>adulterers,</u> nor <u>effeminate</u> nor <u>homosexuals,</u> nor <u>thieves,</u> nor the <u>covetous,</u> nor <u>drunkards,</u> nor <u>revilers,</u> nor <u>swindlers, shall inherit the kingdom of God,</u>

And such were some of you; but you were washed, but you were sanctified, but you were justified in the name of the Lord Jesus Christ and in the Spirit of our God."

Ephesians 5:5-8

"...this you know with certainty, that no immoral or impure person or covetous man who is an idolater, has an inheritance in the kingdom of Christ and God.

Let no one deceive you with empty words, for because of these things the wrath of God comes upon the sons of disobedience. Therefore do not be partakers with them: for you were formerly darkness, but now you are light in the Lord; walk in the light as children of light."

Hebrews 13:4 NASB

"Let marriage be held in honor among all, and let the marriage bed be undefiled; for fornicators and adulterers God will judge."

Romans 1:18-32

"For <u>the wrath of God is revealed from heaven against all ungodliness and unrighteousness of men, who suppress the truth in unrighteousness, because that which is known about God is evident within them, for God made it evident to them.</u>

For since the creation of the world His invincible attributes, His eternal power and divine nature have been clearly seen, being understood through what has been made, so that they are without excuse.

For even though they know God, they did not honor Him as God, or give Him thanks, but they became futile in their speculations and their foolish heart was darkened.

Professing to be wise, they became fools ....

Therefore God gave them over in the lusts of their hearts to impurities, that their bodies might be dishonored among them.

*For **they exchanged the truth of God for a lie, and worshiped and served the creature rather than the Creator,** who is blessed forever. Amen.*

For this reason God gave them over to degrading passions; for their women exchanged the natural function** for that which is unnatural, and **in the same way also the men abandoned the natural function** of the woman and burned in their desire toward one another, men with men **committing indecent acts and receiving in their own persons the due punishment of their error.

*And just **as they did not see fit to acknowledge God any longer, God gave them over to a depraved mind,** to do those things which are not proper, being filled with all unrighteousness, wickedness, greed, malice, full of envy, murder, strifr, deceit, malice; they are gossips, slanderers, haters of God, insolent, arrogant, boastful, inventors of evil, disobedient to parents, without understanding, untrustworthy, unloving, unmerciful, and **although they know the ordinance of God, that those who practice such things are worthy of death, they not only do the*** *same, but also give hearty approval to those who practice them."*

Hebrews 10:26-27

"For if we go on sinning willfully after receiving the knowledge of the truth, there no longer remains a sacrifice for sins, but a certain terrifying expectation of judgment, and THE FURY OF A FIRE WHICH WILL CONSUME THE ADVERSARIES."

Revelation 22:10-15

"... Do not seal up the words of the prophecy of this book .... Let the one who does wrong, still do wrong; and let the one who is filthy still be filthy; and let the one who is righteous still be righteous; and let the one who is holy still be holy." 'Behold, I am coming quickly, and My reward is with Me, to render to every man according to what he has done. I am the Alpha and the Omega, the first and the last, the beginning and the end

Blessed are those who wash their robes, that they may have the right to the tree of life, and may enter by the gates into the city,

<u>Outside are the</u> dogs and the sorcerers and the <u>immoral persons and the murderers and the idolaters, and everyone who loves and practices lying.</u>'"

Our study asks, "How Can I Win?" These verses clearly warn us to pay close attention to every word of the Book of Revelation, so we will.

Looking Again, More Carefully
What Does The Book of Revelation Say about Itself?

Revelation 1:1 Amplified Study Bible
"This is the revelation of Jesus Christ...."

What a subject! Could there be anything or anybody more important for us to know than our Creator and Savior who loves us perfectly? And do we need to know what His true love looks like in these end times and how we are to respond to Him if we want to win?

Now Let's Look at Some Biblical Characters Who Did Win, Eternally

The Thief on the Cross

Probably, few people in heaven have come as close to hell as this thief did, hanging on the cross next to Jesus..

As he hung there in his own personal agony and horror, with no hope for salvation, he listened to Jesus crying out to His Father, not for Himself, but for His enemies and murderers! He was concerned for the salvation of His worst enemies and cried out for His Father to forgive them because they did not know the full magnitude of what they were doing.

The thief had to wonder, "Who is this man? What kind of man, suffering like I am on this hellish cross, is concerned more about his murderers than Himself? "

"Surely, He truly is the Son of God!"

"This salvation thing must be real! And is it truly possible that I can be eternally saved, even at almost my last moment before all hope is eternally gone? What do I have to lose?"

So, after rebuking the other thief for railing against Jesus and declaring that Jesus was truly innocent, but neither he nor the other thief were, he asked, "Jesus, remember me when you come into Your Kingdom!"

And the rest is history! Jesus replied with eternity in His voice, "Truly I say to you, "Today you will be with Me in Paradise!" And he was! Hallelujah!

The Woman at the Well

John 41-45

I love this story of one whose life was totally changed because she went to the well to get physical water, met Jesus there and left full of living water that transformed her life.

Jesus got her attention by revealing Himself to her as a prophet who saw all about her life without condemning her. So, she was not afraid to take the conversation to a whole different level and share her interest in the coming Messiah she had heard about. When He revealed to her that He is the Messiah she was waiting for, she instantly believed because He had already manifested His supernatural gifting to her.

But the thing that excites me even more than her salvation is that she immediately started manifesting her spiritual gifting. Listen to what she did and the results:

John 4:25-30; 39-42

"So <u>the woman left her waterpot and went into the city, and said to the men</u>, 'Come and see a man who told me all the things that I have done; this is not the Christ, is it?' They went..."

(Now listen to the fruit of her manifesting her newfound gift of evangelism through the power of Holy Spirit:)

"And from that city many of the Samaritans believed in Him because of the woman who testified, "He told me all the things I have done." So, when the Samaritans came to Him, they were asking Him to stay with them, and He stayed .... And many more believed because of His word; and they were saying to the woman, 'It is no longer because of what you said that we believe, for we have heard for ourselves and know that this One is indeed the Savior of the world'"

If you are still feeling convicted by the scary Scriptures we read earlier, be encouraged by how easy it was for this woman to repent and be totally **transformed from harlot to evangelist. You, too, can repent, believe and be anointed to be who you were created to be in moments with the help of Holy Spirit power of God in your life right now!**

Peter Who Denied Jesus Three Times

I love the story of Peter, too. He is so real in his desire to follow his Lord, but he suffered from "foot in mouth disease" emotionally and verbally. His understandable fears during the time of Jesus' arrest and crucifixion caused him to feel that he could never be forgiven for denying Jesus 3 times.

But God! But repentance! But transformation by encounters with Jesus after his fall! But Holy Spirit Baptism! But newfound obedience as the leader he was called to be! But becoming the first apostolic leader to be used to birth the New Testament Church in Jerusalem on Pentecost when Holy Spirit fell!

We see how he changed into a wonderfully humble servant of our Lord when he was crucified for his faith. He not only did not deny his Lord to save his life, but he chose to be crucified upside down because he did not see himself worthy of dying like His Lord.

Saul Who Became Paul, the Apostle to the Gentiles

Saul who became Paul the apostle is one of the most interesting church fathers in the Bible. He began as one of the worst enemies of Jesus' followers! He was highly educated as a Pharisee and is recorded in the Bible as being present and in agreement with the stoning of Steven. (Acts 7:57-8:1)

"... Saul began to destroy the church. Going from house to house,

he dragged off both men and women and put them in prison"
(Acts 8:3)

He was one of the worst enemies of Jesus' church until he
had a supernatural encounter with Him!

But God! He saw to it that Saul was dramatically transformed, saved, and delivered, on the road to Damascus.[31]
Jesus struck Saul down to the ground on the road , confronted him, saying, "Saul, why are you persecuting Me? I
am Jesus whom you are persecuting, but rise and enter the
city, and it shall be told you what you must do."

After three days of blindness and no food, God had his attention. He sent his servant Ananias to lay hands on Saul
to heal his eyes. He also was filled with the Holy Spirit and
baptized.

With this and many more encounters with Jesus, Saul became Paul the apostle who is responsible for the gospel
going to the Gentiles and the writing of much of the New
Testament. Paul, too was martyred for his faith, by behead-
ing. But he will be with Jesus and all believers forever.

I hope that this short visit into the stories of 4 people who
had dramatic encounters with the Lord that totally transformed their eternal lives will encourage all who read this
book, so that if you are concerned about your relationship
with the Lord at this moment, you will truly repent of your
sins and iniquities and believe that Jesus is your Savior
and Lord

---

31. Acts 9

I look forward to being a part of The Great Cloud of Witnesses along with these saints of old during The Great Tribulation and forever and forever with our LORD! I **Hope to see You <u>All</u> there!**

ABOUT THE AUTHOR

Dr. Bettye Lundquist began her professional journey in the field of biochemistry, initially trained and educated to become a professor. However, she felt a strong conviction to set aside her academic career in order to devote herself to raising her two daughters during their formative years. During that season, she also taught piano to about 20 students at a time, contributing to her family's needs while nurturing others through music.

Later, she experienced a profound spiritual calling that redirected the course of her life. Led by the Lord, Dr. Lundquist returned to school—not in the traditional academic sense, but through immersive, hands-on spiritual training. She earned Master's and Doctorate degrees with concentrations in Spiritual Warfare, Deliverance, Counseling, and Prophecy. These studies were not merely intellectual exercises; they were deeply experiential and transformative, bringing profound healing from a traumatic childhood marked by satanic ritual abuse and exploitation.

Rather than rushing through her education, she embraced a process of personal deliverance and restoration, committed to discovering her God-ordained identity and purpose beyond victimization. Her journey of healing became a foundation for helping others.

Dr. Lundquist's unique path has taken her around the world. She spent several months in India ministering deliverance to Christian women suffering from spiritual and sexual abuse tied to Hindu practices. She has also been trained in city-reaching and land healing, conducting intercessory missions in places like Argentina and Rome. In the United States, she has led numerous prayer journeys focused on healing Native American communities affected by the historical trauma of the Trail of Tears, as well as land assignments in regions such as Northern Ireland.

Today, Dr. Bettye Lundquist is a teacher, author, and counselor. She ministers personal deliverance, mentors others in spiritual freedom, and equips believers to pursue the fullness of their destiny in Christ—whom she intimately knows as her Lord, Perfect Love, and Bridegroom.

www.ingramcontent.com/pod-product-compliance
Lightning Source LLC
Chambersburg PA
CBHW081926120726
47997CB00010B/3055